Cognitive Harmony

Cognitive Harmony

THE ROLE OF SYSTEMIC HARMONY IN THE CONSTITUTION OF KNOWLEDGE

Nicholas Rescher

UNIVERSITY OF PITTSBURGH PRESS

Published by the University of Pittsburgh Press, Pittsburgh, PA 15260
Copyright © 2005, University of Pittsburgh Press
Manufactured in the United States of America
Printed on acid-free paper
10 9 8 7 6 5 4 3 2 1

Library of Congress Cataloging-in-Publication Data
Rescher, Nicholas.
Cognitive harmony : the role of systemic harmony in the constitution of knowledge /
Nicholas Rescher.
p. cm.
Includes bibliographical references and index.
ISBN 0-8229-4243-7 (hardcover : alk. paper)
1. Knowledge, Theory of.   2. System theory.   3. Cognition.   4. Harmony
(Philosophy).   5. Induction (Logic).   6. Inference.   I. Title.
BD161.R4693 2004
121—dc22
2004021547

For Dale Jacquette

Contents

Preface

The idea of harmony is a key philosophical part of the intellectual legacy bequeathed to us by the ancient Greeks. Usually it is construed in relation to human affairs and interactions. (An eighteenth-century German religious sect known as the "Harmonists" founded a utopian community only an hour's drive from where I now reside in Pittsburgh.) But it also plays a role in purely theoretical matters, and its role in relation to our knowledge of the world is the object of concern in these pages.

Cognitive Harmony has grown out of a lecture I was invited though in the end was unable to give in Germany in 2001 under the auspices of the Brauers Foundation of Baden Baden. I am grateful to Estelle Burris for her multifaceted help in moving the project from my hen-scratches into print.

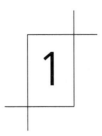

The Systemic Harmony of Fact

Harmony

While *harmony* strikes the modern ear as primarily a musical term, the basic idea it conveys is something far larger both in its origins and in its subsequent history. Its Greek root, *harmonia*, denotes a joining together of components so that the resulting whole can accomplish its natural mission—the planks of a ship, for example, or the bones of a skeleton.[1] And in a still generally similar way the classic second edition of *Webster's Unabridged Dictionary* defines *harmony* in its subsequent, more general sense as "a combination of parts into an orderly whole . . . [exhibiting an] agreement or proportionate arrangement that is pleasing . . . [through] fitting well together." What is at issue throughout is thus a unifying coordination of elements into a comprehensive and evaluatively positive structure—an organically unified whole that is able to realize a positive function through the coordinated collaboration of its several parts.[2] The crux of harmony is a whole whose parts exhibit mutual accommodation under the aegis of normative principles.

The paradigm of harmony is, of course, musical harmony—the coordinated combining of different voices in producing an overall effect (*Einklang,* or a sounding as one). *E pluribus unum* could also be the motto of harmony.

One salient feature of a harmonious whole is thus what might be termed its *systemic integrity*. The crux here is the due coordination of multilateral—and even seemingly conflicting—factors to produce a commonly engendered overall effect.[3] A change that occurs in a harmonious whole becomes diffused throughout: here, when one thing is altered, everything is affected—change something, and nothing else can continue to make its contribution to the whole as effectively as before. Change in a harmonious whole is disequilibration. Were any part of such a whole to be removed—or even merely altered in some significant way—its unity would be disturbed and its evaluative condition diminished; its integrity would be impaired in the wake of any diminution—and thereby its positivity as well. By their very nature, genuinely harmonious wholes are best off as they are—a holism both of being and of value is operative here.

With a harmony, two factors accordingly become crucial: a coordinative unification of component parts and an evaluatively positive overall result, that is, a union of constituents into a functionally unified, coherently integrated whole in a way that is evaluatively positive either by way of intellectual appreciation or of affective response. The former factor might be characterized as *systemic integrity* and the second as *evaluative positivity*. Taken together these are what a *harmony* is all about. Apart from music, other paradigm examples of harmonious wholes are, on the affective side, works of fine art and, on the intellectual/cognitive side, the elegant systematization of bodies of mathematics or of theory manifolds in natural science.

The idea of harmony became significant as a philosophical concept in the thought of Pythagoras and his school in classical antiquity. For the Pythagoreans, the elegant axiomatic unity of geometry represented the quintessence of cognitive harmony and that of music the quintessence of aesthetic harmony. And the two were fused in the functioning of a mathematicized characterization of the motion of the heavenly bodies that made for celestial harmony, the "music of the spheres." The Pythagoreans carried this idea over into medicine as well.

Modern scholars generally characterize a system as a collection of interrelated entities, the relationships among which are such that information about them affords a basis for inferring conclusions about the structure, modus operandi, or temporal history of the system as a whole.[4] Such a formula indicates the plurality of key features of a system: wholeness, interrelatedness of parts, functional interrelationships, all of which are present in the traditional explication of the idea. The concept of systemic harmony is itself a chain that links together many distinguishable elements into a harmonious whole. And because systemic unity is a crucial aspect of any stably perduring whole, it is no wonder that the concept of harmony has penetrated into the thought of virtually every advanced culture on nearly every complex topic.

The Systemic Integrity of Fact and Burley's Principle

Let us now narrow our focus from harmony in general to *cognitive harmony*, characteristically conceived of as the systemic manifold of truth or fact. Facts must be both compatible and consonant with one another; both consistency and coherence are necessary: facts are related in such a way that *each fact not only accommodates all the others but also interconnects into an integrated whole.* For the facts that our beliefs purport often are and ideally always should be united in a pervasively integrated systemic structure. Every determinable fact is so severely hemmed in by others that even when we erase one, it can always be restored on the basis of what remains. The domain of fact is a logical harmony: even if we abandon a particular fact, it could still be effectively recovered from this collection of others. And the reason for this lies in the logical principle of *the systemic integrity of fact,* for the fabric of fact is woven tightly: it is *inferentially redundant;* any given fact can be recovered by logical inference from others in its informative environment.

One of the ways of exhibiting the systemic integrity of fact runs as follows. Assume (as a worst case of sorts) that we are given n truths that are entirely independent of one anther: $p_1, p_2, \ldots p_n$. Then, of course, their overall conjunction, p_1 and p_2 and $\ldots$ and p_n, must also state a true fact. But now consider the propositional set of truths:

$$S = \{p_1, p_2, \ldots p_n, p_1 \text{ and } p_2 \text{ and } \ldots \text{ and } p_n\}$$

Clearly, this is a set of true facts. But observe that this set is such that if any one member were to be deleted it could at once be restored by logical inference from the rest. Their inferential density along such lines means that facts are so closely intermeshed with one another as to form a logical network. Any change anywhere reverberates everywhere; when we fiddle with individual elements of such a system, we endanger the entire whole. In his influential *Treatise on Obligations* the medieval scholastic philosopher Walter Burley (ca. 1275–1345) laid down the rule—let us call it Burley's principle: *Whenever a false contingent proposition is posited, one can prove any false proposition that is compatible with it.*[5] His reasoning was as follows:

Let the facts be that
P. You are not in Rome.
Q. You are not a bishop.

And now, of course, also that
R. You are not in Rome or you are a bishop. (*P* or not-*Q*)

All of these, so we suppose, are true. Let us now posit by way of a (false) supposition that
Not-(*P*) You are in Rome.

Obviously (*P*) must now be abandoned—"by hypothesis." But nevertheless from (R) and not-(*P*) we obtain
You are a bishop. (Not-*Q*)

And in view of thesis (*Q*) this is, of course, false. Thus, given a falsity, that is, not-(*P*)—we have obtained not-(*Q*) by cogent inference from acknowledged truths—where Q is an *arbitrary true proposition*. And it is clear that this situation prevails in general. For let *p* and *q* be any two (arbitrary but nonequivalent) facts. Then all of the following facts will also, of course, result: $\sim(\sim p)$, $p \& q$, $p \vee q$, $p \vee \sim q \vee r$, $\sim p \vee q$, $\sim(\sim p$ and *q*), and so on. Let us focus on just three of these available facts:
1. *p*
2. *q*
3. $\sim(\sim p \& q)$ or, equivalently, $p \vee \sim q$

Now let it be that you are going to suppose not-p. Then, of course, you must remove (1) from the list of accepted facts and substitute

(1′) ~p

But there is now no stopping. For together with (3) this new item at once yields ~q, contrary to (2). Thus, that supposition of ours that runs contrary to accepted fact (that is, not-p) has the direct consequence that *any other arbitrary truth must also be abandoned*.

On this basis Burley's principle has far-reaching implications. For giving the systemic interconnectedness of fact, any and all fact-contradicting assumptions are pervasively destabilizing. As far as the logic of the situation is concerned, you cannot change anything in the domain of fact without endangering everything. Once you embark on a contrary-to-fact assumption, then as far as pure logic is concerned all the usual bets are off. Changing one fact always requires changing others as well.

A concrete illustration will help to make the point more graphic. Consider the situation of x emplaced as follows in a tic-tac-toe configuration:

Here we have the following facts:
1. There is exactly one x in the configuration.
2. This x is not in the first row.
3. This x is not in the third row.
4. This x is not in the second column.
5. This x is not in the third column.
6. This x is not on a diagonal.
7. This x is not at column-row position (3, 2).

Let it be that we erase one of the facts, say (5). Then, as we have already noted, the other facts of the situation will suffice to let us recover this by logical inference.

But now suppose that we do not simply lose sight of (5) by its *era-sure* but actually *change* it, replacing it by not-(5). Then, of course, we would also have to go on to deny either (4) or (7). The fabric of fact is *logically unified:* any change in one fact will always compel further changes in other facts. And so from a logical standpoint the manifold of fact is an integral unit, a harmonious system where nothing can be altered without affecting something else.

This circumstance of the systemic integrity of fact has far-reaching ramifications. It means that once we begin to make alterations in the domain of fact we embark on a process that has no end. Suppose that we make only a very small alteration in the descriptive composition of the real, say, by adding one pebble to the river bank. But which pebble? Where are we to get it and what are we to put in its place at the location we take it from? And where are we to put the air or the water that this new pebble displaces? And when we put that material in a new spot, just how are we to make room for it? And how are we to make room for the material displaced there? Moreover, the region within six inches of the new pebble used to hold N pebbles. It now holds $N + 1$. Of which region are we to say that it holds $N - 1$? If it is that region yonder, then how did the pebble get here from there? By a miraculous instantaneous transport? By a little boy picking it up and throwing it? But, then, which little boy? And how did he get there? And if he threw it, then what happened to the air that his throw displaced that would otherwise have gone undisturbed? Here, problems arise without end. Every hypothetical change in the physical makeup of the real sets in motion a vast cascade of changes either in the physical constitution of the real or in the laws of nature at large, for what about the structure of the envisioning electromagnetic, thermal, and gravitational fields? Just how are these to be preserved as was given the removal and/or shift of the pebbles? How is matter to be readjusted to preserve consistency here? Or are we to do so by changing the fundamental laws of physics?

The systemic integrity of fact indicates that we cannot make hypothetical modifications in the makeup of the real without thereby destabilizing everything and raising an unending series of questions. And not only do *redistributions* raise problems but so do even mere *erasures,* mere cancellations, because reality being as it is requires that redistributions follow in their wake. If by hypothesis we zap that book on the shelf out of existence, then what is it that supports the others? And at what stage of its history did the book first disappear? And if the book just vanished a moment ago, then what of the law of the conservation of matter? And whence the material that is now in that book-denuded space? Once more, we embark on an endless journey. As such considerations indicate, it is difficult to exaggerate the larger significance and import of the systemic harmony of fact.

Some Aspects of Cognitive Harmony

The object of the cognitive enterprise is to devise a manifold of putative truth that reflects, as clearly as possible, the developments of the manifold of fact. After all, inquiry is the pursuit of *truth.* And the overall domain of truth is in itself clearly a system—*das System der Wahrheiten überhaupt,* as Lambert called it.[6]

Let us consider the way in which the idea that "truth is a system" is to be understood. Three things are at issue: the set *T* of truths must have the features of *comprehensiveness* (or completeness), *consistency,* and *cohesiveness* (unity). The first two are familiar and well understood. Let us concentrate on the third.[7] Thus, when we formulate our knowledge claims systematically, we are endowing them with *verisimilitude* in its root sense of "resemblance to the truth." One arrives at the inference:

KNOWLEDGE MUST REFLECT THE TRUTH.

THE TRUTH IS A SYSTEM.

KNOWLEDGE SHOULD BE A SYSTEM.

This idea—that if our truth claims are indeed to approximate the truth itself, then they too must be capable of systematic development—has historically provided one of the prime grounds for adopting the systematicity of knowledge as a regulative ideal.

Against this background, it is only normal, natural, and to be expected that cognitive theory should insist that the standing of our knowledge should reflect the systemic harmony of fact insofar as such a parallelism is at all realizable.

From antiquity to Hegel and beyond, cognitive theoreticians have embraced the ancient ideal that our knowledge should be developed architectonically and should be organized within an articulated structure that exhibits the linkages binding its component parts into an integrated whole and leaves nothing wholly isolated and disconnected. A cognitive system is to provide a framework for linking the *disjecta membra* of the bits and pieces of our knowledge into a cohesive unity. A cognitive system is to be a *structured* body of information, one that is organized in accordance with taxonomic and explanatory principles that link this information into a rationally coordinated whole.[8] The functional categories governing this organizational venture are those of understanding, explanation, and cognitive rationalization.

The underlying idea of a unity of knowledge has found many forms of expression over the course of time. The encyclopedia as a synoptic compendium of knowledge is historically its prime literary expression. And the university as an educational enterprise is historically its prime institutional expression. On the contemporary scene, its prime manifestation is the Internet with its powerful (though still rudimentary) search engines for effecting a coordination of information.

What counts for a cognitive system is the explanatory connection of ideas, not the particular style or format of their presentation. A system is individuated through general features relating to its structure and its rational architectonic, not through the particular manner of its expository development. Cognitive systematization is thus an epistemological notion, not a literary or rhetorical one—a matter of the organization of information, not its mode of presentation; of explanation, not of exposition.

The idea of systematization is intimately intertwined with that of planning in its generic sense of the rational organization of materials.[9] Planning, like organizing, is a mode of intellectual action, and it too exhibits the "amphibious" character of systematization. On the physical side one can have such projects as town planning, architecture, and landscape gardening; on the cognitive side, one can plan the organization for the purpose of explanatory or deductive or dialectical (persuasive) or mnemonic codification. Again, systematization is closely connected with the enterprise of design, albeit with a difference in orientation. For design—as generally understood—aims at the realization of physical forms,[10] while systematization is not less concerned with intellectual ones. But the basic issues are the same on both sides: the articulation of a rational structure on the basis of "best-fit" considerations, with all the parameters of systematization—economy, efficiency, generality, uniformity, and so on—figuring in this role. A cognitive system is a "design for knowing," and system building is preeminently a problem of rational design.

A painting or piece of architecture—any good design—must combine a variety of potentially conflicting elements in the conjoining synthesis of a cooperative harmony, and this sort of rational unification is exactly what a system is all about. The harmonious systematicity of knowledge is thus to be construed as a category of understanding, akin in this regard to generality, simplicity, and elegance. Its immediate concern is with form rather than matter, and it bears on the organizational development of our knowledge rather than on the substantive content of what is known, and deals with cognitive structure rather than subject-matter materials. Just as one selfsame range of things can be characterized simply or complexly, so it can be characterized systematically or unsystematically. Systematicity relates in the first instance not to *what* we know—the facts at issue in the information at our disposal—but rather to *how we proceed in organizing our knowledge*. And these two issues are, of course, going to be closely interrelated.

The Functions of Cognitive Systematization

The truth about reality must inevitably form a system, but this is more than can be said for our *knowledge* of it. Cognitive harmony consists in systematization—in fusing the sundry bits and pieces of our knowledge into a cohesively structured and rationally integrated whole. It constitutes an ideal for the rational articulation of our knowledge—alike in its formal and its factual subdomains. However, it is well to begin by recognizing that there is no justification for issuing in advance—prior to any furtherance of the enterprise itself—a categorical assurance that the effort to systematize our knowledge of the world is bound to succeed. The systematicity of our factual knowledge is not something that can be guaranteed a priori, as prevailing on the basis of the "general principles" of the matter. The parameters of systematicity—coherence, consistency, uniformity, and the rest—represent a family of regulative ideals toward whose realization our cognitive endeavors do and should strive. But the drive for systematicity is the operative expression of a guiding aim or objective and thus not something whose realization can be taken for granted as already certain and settled from the start. There is no valid reason to assume or presume from the very outset that systematicity will ultimately emerge in the results of our inquires. The best we can do here is to proceed in the light of a hope that we expect the wisdom of hindsight to validate eventually.

This drive for cognitive order and cohesion is informed and crucially conditioned by a coordinate cognitive drive for comprehensiveness, variety, novelty, and the like. As students of human biology have shrewdly observed, the central nervous system of humans demands a novelty of inputs to avoid boredom—exploratory behavior and novelty-tropism are a fundamental aspect of the biological outfitting of higher animals.[11] Clearly, the systematization of our knowledge of fact has a deep Darwinian rationalization. To make our way in a difficult world, we humans, as rational animals, need to exploit regularities for our effective functioning. Now, the rules and principles of rational procedure are easiest to grasp, master, to apply, and to transmit if they themselves are organized in as a rational structure, that is, are developed systematically. And the concern for system is nothing else than this drive for metarulishness, an effort to impart to our principles of behavioral and intellectual procedure a structure that is itself a manifold integrated by systemic principles.

A cognitive system is not just a collection of endorsed (or accepted) *theses* but also embodies the *rationale* that underwrites these endorsements. The characterization of a system-included thesis in normative terms (as "true," "warrantedly assertible," and the like) is the product of the operations of rationale-establishing principles that are no less crucial to the makeup of the system than the theses it accommodates. Christian Wolff's formula applies: a cognitive system as "a collection of truths duly arranged in accordance with the principles governing their connection" (*systema est varbartum inter se et cum principiis suis connexarum congeries*).[12]

But the question remains: what rational considerations render systematicity so desirable—what is the legitimative grounding of its status as a regulative ideal in cognition? What, in short, does systematicity do for us? After all, systematization is a purposeful action and "system" is a functional concept—systematizing is something that has to have a purpose to it. The answer here is straightforward. Knowledge is organized with various ends in view—in particular, the heuristic (to make it easier to learn, retain, and utilize) and the probative (to test and thereby render it better supported and more convincing). *Homo sapiens* as a rational animal exhibits a deep need for understanding, and the facets of rational structure (unity, comprehensiveness, coherence, and the rest) are constitutive components of that systematicity through which alone understanding can be achieved.

This epistemological dimension will be our prime focus of concern. In the present study of cognitive systematization it will, in effect, be the monograph and not the textbook that is the paradigm. We shall put aside the psychological aspects of knowledge acquisition and utilization (learning, remembering, and so on), focusing instead on the rational aspects of organizing knowledge in its probative and explanatory dimensions. We shall deal with the systematizing of knowledge as a matter of cognitive planning for theoretical and purely cognitive purposes rather than focusing on matters of learning and training.

Given such a focus on probative and explanatory issues, the systematic development of knowledge—or purported knowledge—may be seen to serve three interrelated functions:

1. *Intelligibility:* Systematicity is the prime vehicle for understanding, for what renders factual claims intelligible is their systematic interrelationships. As long as they remain discrete and disconnected, they lack any adequate handle for the intellect that

seeks to take hold of them in its endeavor to comprehend the issues involved.

2. *Rational organization:* Systematicity—in its concern for such desiderata as simplicity and uniformity—affords the means to a probatively rational and scientifically viable articulation and organization of our knowledge; the systematic development of knowledge is thus a key part of the idea of a science.

3. *Verification:* Systematicity is a vehicle of cognitive quality control. It is plausible to suppose that systematically developed information is more likely to be correct—or at any rate less likely to be defective—thanks to its avoidance of the internal error-indicative conflicts of discrepancy, inconsistency, and disuniformity. This indicates the service of systematization as a testing process for acceptability, an instrument of verification.

Let us consider these three themes more closely. Its commitment to providing a rationale renders cognitive systematization an indispensable instrument of rationality. Within a systematic framework, the information to be organized is brought within the control of a network of rule-governed explanatory and justificatory relationships. The facts are thus placed within patterns of order through their subordination under common principles, and their explanatory rationalization is accordingly facilitated. Systematicity is the key to understanding—it provides the channels through which explanatory power flows.

Cognitive systematization thus constitutes an instrumentality explanation, and we explain things with an end in view—namely, to make them intelligible. And this calls for a discernment of rationally available patterns, rendering matters "only natural and to be expected" through the provision of a suitable rationale. A systematic synthesis on the basis of evidential or explanatory cohesion does the job of "accounting for" the theses at issue in both senses of this term—that is, to explain the fact and to provide grounds for its claims to factuality. In this way, a cognitive system provides illumination: the systematic interconnectedness of facts render those at issue amenable to reason by setting them within a framework of ordering principles that bring their mutual interrelationships to light. But what is the nature of the interconnecting linkages at issue here?

The two main possibilities for rational linkage are connections of the probative or *evidential* order and connections of the justificatory or *explanatory* order. There is an important difference here between these two. In the latter case we are concerned with what medieval schoolmen called the order of why-it-is-so reasons (*rationes essendi,* or ontological reasons), and in the former with what they called why-we-hold-it-to-be-so reasons (*rationes cognoscendi,* or epistemological reasons). Consider the height of yonder tree. I say it is roughly one hundred feet high. The ontological reason for my claim will lie in the following sort of explanation: that it is a tree of such-and-such sort, which has such-and-such growth characteristics. And that the soil and weather conditions afforded it with such-and-such requisites for growth. On the other hand, the epistemological reason for my claim might simply be that it cast a shadow of approximately ten feet at a time when a certain ten-foot pole cast a shadow of one foot. The one set of reasons deals with the *explanation* of our claims, the other with how we *substantiate* them—our rationale *for our holding them to be so.*

But notwithstanding the distinction that is at work, there need be no separation here. For in the end the best basis for evidentiation—for substantiating a claim—is through an understanding of why it is in the larger scheme of things that the claimed fact must be so. Substantiation should cohere with substance. And, so, the very fact that a certain item fits neatly into an explanatory system provides a powerful indication that we have gotten it right and affords us with substantial evidence for this claim.

The systematic development of our knowledge accordingly provides us with a test of cognitive appropriateness; it serves as a monitor of the adequacy of the articulation of our body of knowledge (or purported knowledge). This is evident from a consideration of the very nature of the various parameters of systematicity: consistency, consonance, coherence—and even completeness (comprehensiveness). The advantages of injecting these factors into the organizing articulation of our knowledge are virtually self-evident. In the pursuit of factual knowledge we strive to secure correct information about the world. We accordingly endeavor to reject falsehoods, striving to ensure that to the greatest feasible extent the wrong theses are kept out of our range of cognitive commitments. And the pursuit of consistency, consonance, coherence, and completeness clearly facilitates the attainment of this ruling objective. The systematization of knowledge is a prime instrument of error-avoidance—of cognitive quality control.

There are in fact very different sorts of "errors." There are errors of omission, which arise when we do not accept the statement P when P is in fact the case. These involve the sanction (disvalue) of ignorance. And there are errors of commission, which arise when we accept P when in fact not-P is the case. These involve the mark of cognitive dissonance and outright mistake. And clearly both sorts of missteps are errors. The rules of the cognitive game call not only for rejecting falsehoods and keeping the wrong things out but also for accepting truths and assuring that the right things get in. Systematization is a great help in these regards. It is presumptively error-minimizing with respect to the two kinds of cognitive errors. Given its coordinated stress on comprehensiveness and mutual fit, the systematization of our knowledge clearly facilitates the realization of its governing objective: the engrossing of information in the context of an optimal balance of truth over falsehoods.

An effective cognitive system must be constructed more like a medieval trail than a modern highway. It must follow the natural bends and contours of the terrain that it traverses rather than cutting a level path through it all. A good system must afford a vivid look over its landscape as it stands rather than reshaping that landscape to suit its own convenience. Again, those parameters of systematization must themselves be balanced on systematic harmony. Achieving simplicity, say, through sacrificing comprehensiveness by arbitrarily dismissing inconvenient detail, is a pathway not to supersystematicity but to a betrayal of the systemic enterprise as such.

The Value Dimension

At this point the reader may well feel tempted to interject as follows:

The preceding discussion has insisted on the harmony of the domain of fact. But as was stipulated from the very outset, harmony requires both systemic integrity and evaluative positivity. Granted, the discussion has shown in some detail that the factual realm entails systemic integrity by way of inferential interconnection. But this axiological aspect of the matter yet remains untouched. This comment is quite in order and it is now time to remedy this omission.

The evaluative dimension here is rooted in the nature of the systemic integrity at issue. For in this factual arena it is not just a system that is at issue but a *cognitive* system—one whose very integrity is rooted in inferential principles of logical interconnection. It is this logical coherence of fact—the circumstance of it admitting a smooth inferential transit from place to place within the overall domain—that facilitates comprehension. Systematicity facilitates cognitive access: a systemic whole of inferentially interrelated fact is for this very reason user friendly for rational intelligences engaged in the quest for understanding.

The evaluative aspect of factual harmony is accordingly grounded in the circumstance that the realm of fact is not only a systemically cohesive unit under the aegis of principles but that the principles at work here are themselves the fundamental principles of rational cognition. But cognition itself is a prime human good. And rationality is a deeply normative conception in which all of the characteristic cognitive virtues of a *system* of propositions—unity, coherence, simplicity, and the rest—play a prominent role. All of these, after all, are so many modes of intellectual economy and elegance that render the body of knowledge at issue user friendly to a mind seeking to understand and master it. All such fashions are "aesthetic" aspects of a body of information that facilitate its comprehensibility. Accordingly, any intelligent being committed to rational comprehension is bound to prize these features of cognitive systematicity. For intelligent beings, comprehensibility and intelligibility are automatically bound to count as cardinal virtues because they render the materials at issue grist to its mill. Systems as such can be good or bad; but *cognitive* systems can by their very nature lay some claim to positivity. In sum, in the case of a specifically cognitive system it is the factor of systemic integrity itself that provides for the positivity that is requisite for a harmonious whole.

This value dimension of a cognitive system—the infusion of value into the realm of fact through the mediation of its comprehensibility—was already at work in the teaching of Plato. The following passage from the *Timaeus* clearly attests to this:

> The world is the best of things that have become and its course is the best of courses. Having come to be, then, in this way, the world has been fashioned on the model of that which is comprehensible by rational discourse and understanding. . . . The demiurge [world-maker] brought the world from disorder into order, since he judged that order was in every way the better. . . . Wishing to make this world most closely like that intelligible order which is best and in every way complete . . . its maker did not . . . [make several] but this cosmos has come to be and is and shall hereafter be one and unique. . . . [On this basis] the body of the universe was brought into being, coming into concord (*philia*) by means of proportion (*analogia*). (*Timaeus* 32 B.C.)[13]

In just this same way, the cosmogenesis of Book 10 of Plato's *Republic* pictures creative Necessity as compiling a single unified rational harmony (*harmonia*)—explicitly so characterized. And throughout the history of neo-Platonism this aspect of interconnected coherence of fact and reality remained in the foreground. "All things conspire together" (*sympnoia panta*) was a central thesis of Plotinus.

In any event, cognitive systematicity, however, occupies a different situation. Its status as a regulative ideal is inherent in the very nature of the cognitive enterprise. For the key aspects of system—that is, comprehensiveness and order—engender a native aspect that inheres in the very nature of humans' cognitive position as a creature emplaced *in medias res* in a world not of our making, and hostile or at best indifferent, that we must bring under cognitive control.

Systematic Harmonization in the Cognitive System Concept Itself

It is clear that harmonious systematicity is itself a systemically fact-coordinative concept that unites in a symbiotic and systemic union various elements that, from the purely theoretical perspective, might well go their separate ways, but which "the ways of the world"—or, rather, the conceptualizing mechanisms that afford our instrumentalities for their rationalizations—have inseparably joined together.

The parameters of systematicity (simplicity, regularity, uniformity, comprehensiveness, cohesiveness, unity, harmony, economy, and so on) all represent certain intellectual values or norms within the cognitive enterprise. To be sure, this fact that systematicity involves a coordinated plurality of desiderata means that these may possibly conflict with one another in concrete contexts. The pluralism of desiderata—the fact that each must be taken in the context of others within the overall picture of systematicity—means that their pursuit must moderate them to one another. Whenever multiple desiderata interact, we cannot appropriately cultivate one without reference to the rest. For when we have to evaluate something where different, incommensurable, and potentially conflicting value parameters are at work, the issue is no longer one of maximization but one of harmonization, of getting a balance that, when all is considered, achieves optimality without necessarily maximizing each of those parameters.[14] Harmonious balance is the key here.

Consider an analogy: The prime desideratum in a motor car is its safety. But it would not do to devise a "perfectly safe" car that only goes 1.75 miles per hour. Safety, speed, efficiency, operating economy, breakdown-avoidance are *all* prime desiderata of a motor car. Each counts, but none predominates at the expense of another. A good car design incorporates them all. The situation with respect to our cognitive ideals is altogether parallel. In formulating an effective cognitive system in a particular case, achieving completeness may require sacrificing simplicity. The need for mutual support and functional unity may countervail against functional elegance and economy. In the cognitive systematization of a certain body of knowledge the various parameters of systematization—simplicity, uniformity, comprehensiveness, and the rest—may represent focuses of conflict and tension.

Systematicity is an internally complex and multicriterial conception that embraces and synthesizes all the various aspects of an organic, functionally harmonious whole. The paradigmatic system is a whole that has subordinate parts whose existence and functioning facilitate—indeed, make possible—the existence and functioning of the resulting whole. A true system is subject to a pervasive unity of interrelated components, a unity that correlates with the notion of functional harmony completeness.

Interestingly enough, then, the conception of systematic integrity that is pivotal for harmony is thus itself a system-oriented conception: a whole that represents a congeries of closely interrelated and harmoniously interconnected conceptions. It is a composite idea, a complex Gestalt in which various duly connected, structural elements play a crucial role. The notions of *organism* and *organic unity* provide a unifying center for this range of ideas whose focal point is the harmonious collaboration of mutually supportive parts operating in the interest of a unifying aim or principle.[15]

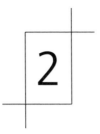

2

Cognitive Harmony in
Historical Perspective

Historical Matters

Cognitive harmony is a matter of systematization. Like anything else, the idea of a "system" has a history, and in this regard the Renaissance gave the term renewed currency. At first it functioned here, too, in its ancient applications in its broad sense of a generic composite. But in due course Protestant theologians of the sixteenth century adopted it to stand specifically for the comprehensive exposition of the articles of faith, along the lines of a medieval *summa:* a doctrinal *compendium.*[1]

By the early years of the seventeenth century, the philosophers had borrowed the term *system* from the theologians, using it to stand for a synoptically comprehensive and connected treatment of a philosophical discipline: logic, rhetoric, metaphysics, ethics, and so on.[2] (It was frequently employed in this descriptive sense in the title of expository books.)[3] And thereafter the term was generalized to apply to such a synoptic treatment of any discipline whatever.[4]

A further development in the use of the term occurred in the second half of the seventeenth century. Now *system* came to be construed as a *particular approach* to a certain subject—a particular theory or doctrine about it as articulated in an organized complex of concordant hypotheses, a *nexus veritatum*. (This new usage is particularly marked in Malebranche's treatise *De la recherche de la vérité* [*De inquirenda veritate libri sex* (Geneva, 1685)], where we find a section *"De novorum systematum inventoribus,"* [devoted to surveying systems].) This is the sense borne by the term in such phrases as "the system of occasional causes" of the Stoic system of morality. Leibniz was a prime promoter of this usage. He often spoke of his own philosophy as "my (new) system" of preestablished harmony, contrasting it with various rival systems.[5] System was now understood as a doctrine or teaching in its comprehensive (that is, "systematic") development. In the wake of this new redeployment of the term in relation to a baroque proliferation of competing doctrines, philosophy now came to be viewed as a battleground of rival systems.

This use of *system* to stand for a comprehensive (if controversial) particular philosophical doctrine opened the idea up to criticism and brought systems into disrepute in the age of reason. Thus Condillac developed a judicious critique of systems in his celebrated *Treatise on Systems*.[6] He distinguished between systems based on *speculation* ("abstract principles," "gratuitous suppositions," "mere hypotheses") and those based on *experience*. A system cannot be better than its underlying principles, and this—he held—invalidates philosophical systems, since they are based on hypotheses along the lines disdained in Isaac Newton's famous dictum: *Hypotheses non fingo*. Scientific systems, on the other hand, were viewed in a very different light. For Condillac, systems can thus be either good or bad—good systems are those that are *scientific,* based on "experience," typified by Newtonian physics; bad ones are those that are *philosophical,* based on speculative hypotheses, typified by the ideas of the pre-Socratics.

The cognitively oriented conception of an *intellectual* system did not by any means totally displace the thing-oriented idea of an *ontological* system—even among the early modern philosophers. For example, throughout most of modern philosophy the most diversely oriented thinkers (Leibniz, Berkeley, Kant, Mill) offer an analysis of *substance*—of physical things—that demands an invocation of the idea of systems to furnish the needed integrating principle. (And this line of approach is no less apposite when what is at issue is a physical *process* rather than a material object—say, a thunderstorm rather than an apple.) The ontological role that is, in effect, accorded to systematicity in much of recent philosophy is not less striking than its key place in the theory of knowledge. The concept has always operated amphibiously, extending over both the physical and the cognitive domains.[7] It is, however, this latter, intellectual side of the issue that will preoccupy us here.

The Traditional View of Cognitive Systems

Cognitive rationality pivots on the idea of systemic harmony. Although the concept of cognitive systematization is very old, the term *system* itself was not used in this sense until much later. In ancient Greek, *systêma* (from *syn-histêmi*, "to [make to] stand together") originally meant something joined together—a connected or composite whole. The term figures in Greek antiquity to describe a wide variety of composite object—such as flocks of animals, medications, military formations, organized governments, poems, and musical configurations.[8] Its technicalization began with the Stoics, who applied it specifically to the physical universe (*systema mundi*)—the composite cosmos encompassing "heaven and earth."[9] What gradually became preeminent is the idea of a system as an organism—an organized whole of interrelated and mutually supportive parts functioning as a cohesive and coherent unit. But the term continued in use throughout classical texts in its very general ordinary sense (which it shared with terms like *syntagma* and *systaxis*.)

Thus, while use of *system* in this way is of relatively recent date, the underlying *idea* of what we nowadays call a "system" of knowledge was certainly alive in classical antiquity, with the Euclidean systematization of geometry providing a paradigm for this conception. In fact, it has been insisted throughout the history of Western philosophy that we do not genuinely *know* something unless this knowledge is actually *systematic*. The general structure of this conception can already be discerned in the pre-Socratics, especially in the seminal thought of Parmenides.[10] Plato's thesis in the *Theaetetus* that a known fact must have a *logos* (rationale), Aristotle's insistence in the *Posterior Analytics* that strict (scientific) knowledge of a fact about the world calls for its accounting in causal terms, the Scholastic analysis of *scientia,* Spinoza's celebration of what he designates as the higher, second, and third kinds of knowledge (in Book III of the *Ethics* and elsewhere), all instantiate the common, fundamental idea that what is genuinely known is known in systemic terms within the larger setting of a rationale-providing framework of explanatory order. Increasingly over the centuries, the idea took hold that there should be a cognitive system organizing the totality of our knowledge into an orderly whole that functions as an "organic" unity.[11] And thus the conception that all truths form one comprehensive and cohesive system in which everything has its logically appropriate place represents one of the many fundamental ideas that the ancient Greeks contributed to the intellectual heritage of the West.

   The post-Renaissance construction of systematicity emphasized its orientation toward specifically *cognitive* or knowledge-organizing systems. The explicit *theory* of such cognitive systems was launched during the second half of the eighteenth century, and the principal theoreticians were two German contemporaries: Johann Heinrich Lambert (1728–1777) and Immanuel Kant (1724–1804). The *practice* of systematization that lay before their eyes was that of the great seventeenth-century philosopher-scientists: Descartes, Spinoza, Newton, Leibniz, and the subsequent workers of the Leibnizian school—especially Christian Wolff. The main use of the system concept with all these later writers relates not to its application to material things but to its specifically *cognitive* applications to the organization of information. Kant puts the matter suggestively as follows:

   In accordance with reason's legislative prescriptions, our diverse modes of knowledge must not be permitted to be a mere rhapsody, but must form a system. Only so can they further the essential ends of reason. By a system I understand the unity of the manifold modes of knowledge under one idea. This idea is the concept . . . [which] determines *a priori* not only the scope of its manifold content, but also the positions which the parts occupy relatively to one another. The scientific concept of reason contains, therefore, the end and the form of that whole which is congruent with this requirement. The unity of the end to which all the parts relate and in the idea of which they all stand in relation to one another, makes it possible for us to determine from our knowledge of the other parts whether any part be missing, and to prevent any arbitrary addition, or in respect of its completeness [to discover] any indeterminateness that does not conform to the limits which are thus determined *a priori.* The whole is thus an organised unity (*articulatio*), and not an aggregate (*coacervatio*). It may grow from within (*per intussusceptionem*), but not by external addition (*per appositionem*). It is thus like an animal body.[12]

Kant further maintains that:

only after we have spent much time in the collection of materials in somewhat random fashion at the suggestion of an idea lying hidden in our minds, and after we have, indeed, over a long period assembled the materials in a merely technical manner, does it first become possible for us to discern the idea in a clearer light, and to devise a while architectonically in accordance with the ends of reason. Systems seem to be formed in the manner of lowly organisms, through a *generatio aequivoca* from the mere confluence of assembled concepts, at first imperfect, and only gradually attaining to completeness, although they one and all have had their schema, as the original germ, in the sheer self-development of reason. Hence, not only is each system articulated in accordance with an idea, but they are one and all organically united in a system of human knowledge, as members of one whole.[13]

Along these lines, Lambert adduced the following examples of diverse cognitive systems: the system of truths at large; individual systems by way of scientific theories; knowledge systems and belief systems of particular cultures or individuals; religious systems, creeds, myths, "symbolic" books; and literary systems, such as narratives, fables, poems, and speeches. Lambert and Kant stressed that the idea of system applied alike to *material* systems (such as organisms) and *intellectual* systems (such as "organically" integrated bodies of knowledge). The idea is neutral as between its material and its cognitive applications.[14] They also clearly recognized that there are physical as well as cognitive systems and, moreover, that systems can lie on the practical as well as the theoretical side and that there can be behavioral systems of rules of procedure, or methods of action, or purposive means or instrumentalities, and so on.

The Modus Operandi of Cognitive Systematization

Traditionally, the two definitive aspects of *system*—the ontological (material) and the cognitive (intellectual)—were seen as closely connected through the conception of truth as *adaequatio intellectu ad rem*. If the objects we study (nature and its components) are systems, then such a parallelism principle dictates the requirement that the intellectual framework we create in the course of this study should itself also be a system. The pre-Kantian ("dogmatic") tradition thus sees a *metaphysical* basis for the imperative to impart to our thought a systematic order akin to that which we find in its objects. With Kant (as we shall see) this imperative to systematization becomes endowed with a strictly epistemological rationale. But however connected or disconnected, these two facets of *system* are both uneliminably *there*.

To be sure, some recent writers urge the need for maintaining a careful line of separation between *intellectual* systems, where systems talk relates to "*formulations* of various kinds that are used for descriptive or conceptual-organizational purposes in science," and *physical* systems as "extra-linguistic entities which, in fact, might be described or referred to by such formulations."[15] But any rigid bifurcation seems ill-advised. It is wrong to think that two different systems concepts are at issue. As our historical considerations show, we are dealing with a deep-rooted parallelism, a pluralized application of one single underlying conception.[16] And, actually, the development of *general* systems theory over the past generation should be seen as an attempt to forge a comprehensive unifying framework within which all of the diverse applications of the systems idea could be accommodated—physical systems (be they natural or artificial), process control systems, and cognitive systems alike.

Lambert contrasted a system with its contraries, all "that one might call a chaos, a mere mixture, an aggregate, an agglomeration, a confusion, an uprooting, etc." ("[*alles*] *was man ein Chaos, ein Gemische, einen Hauffen, einen Klumpen, eine Verwirrung, eine Zerüttung, etc. nennt*").[17] And in synthesizing the discussions of the early theoreticians of the system concept one sees the following features emerge as the definitive characteristics of systematicity:

1. *Wholeness:* unity and integrity as a genuine whole that embraces and integrates its constituent parts
2. *Comprehensiveness:* avoidance of gaps or missing components, inclusiveness with nothing needful left out
3. *Self-sufficiency:* independence, self-containment, autonomy
4. *Cohesiveness:* connectedness, interrelationship, interlinkage, coherence (in one of its senses), a conjoining of the component parts, rules, laws, linking principles; if some components are changed or modified, then others will react to this alteration
5. *Consonance:* consistency and compatibility, coherence (in another of its senses), absence of internal discord or dissonance; harmonious mutual collaboration or coordination of components "having all the pieces fall into place"
6. *Architectonic:* a well-integrated structure of arrangement of duly ordered component parts; generally in an hierarchic ordering of sub- and superordination
7. *Functional unity:* purposive interrelationship; a unifying rationale or telos that finds its expression in some synthesizing principle of functional purport
8. *Functional regularity:* rulishness and lawfulness, orderliness of operation, uniformity, normality (conformity to "the usual course of things")
9. *Functional simplicity:* elegance, harmony and balance, structural economy, tidiness in the collaboration or coordination of components

10. *Mutual supportiveness:* the components of a system are so
    combined under the aegis of a common purpose or principle
    as to conspire together in mutual collaboration for its real-
    ization; interrelatedness
11. *Functional efficacy:* efficiency, effectiveness, adequacy to the
    common task

These are the definite *parameters of systematization.* A system, properly speaking, must exhibit all of these characteristics though not necessarily to the same extent, let alone perfectly. These facets of systematicity reflect matters of degree, and systems can certainly vary in their
embodiment. They are matters of degree that can be realized more or
less fully in various applications of the idea.

On this basis, systematicity has, vis-à-vis its components, the character of a *profile* (rather than an average). Just as the health of a person is determined by a plurality of constituent factors (blood pressure,
white cell count, and so on), so the systematicity of a body of knowledge is determined in terms of a wide variety of separable albeit interrelated considerations. And there will be trade-offs as there are between the various "parameters of systematicity." And so in looking at
alternative systematizations, we must face such questions as whether
the extent to which systematization I outweighs systematization II in
point of parameters B and C suffices to compensate for the extent to
which II outweighs I in point of A. In any concrete application of the
idea to the realization of systematic treatment of some body of claims,
we might have to trade some of these factors for others: greater
completeness may threaten consistency, consistency may endanger
completeness, greater connectedness may require the insertion of dis-
uniform elements, greater uniformity may demand loss of connectedness. Any single parameter of systematization is just one element in
the overall cost/benefit calculations. And, therefore, even if we pursue
our inquiry into nature under the aegis of certain regulative ideals—
such as coherence—we might nevertheless be driven in the final
analysis by systematic considerations to the result that some will be
sacrificed (in part) for the sake of others. Despite our best attempts to
produce, say, a simple picture of nature, we might nevertheless find

that our systematizing efforts themselves force us willy-nilly into a position that fails to yield this desideratum to any substantial extent.

As these deliberations indicate, the systemic harmony of fact is an idea that is as old as Western philosophy itself. To be sure, it has gradually been liberated from the quasi-religious ramifications it had in the days of Pythagoras and Plato. Its present understanding is grounded in logical and epistemological considerations. But notwithstanding this difference in its ideological ramifications, the basic idea that the factual realm constitutes a unified and rationally harmonious manifold, organized and integrated on logical principles, remains what it has ever been—a ruling conception of Western thought.

However, while the idea of the harmonization of fact under the aegis of reason has indeed been prominent throughout the history of Western philosophy, Kant's "Copernican revolution" saw an important reversal here. For once one grants that rational order is coordinated with fact, the question remains: which is the dependent and which the independent variable here? Is the real rational because reality answers to rationality (as somehow the product thereof) or is it so because rationality is answerable to reality as being a prime requisite for its investigator and knower? In the ancien régime of pre-Kantian dogmatism, people thought the former, holding to the ontological view that reason is somehow the creator of fact. But after Kant's Copernican revolution the latter view predominated and reason became the subordinate client of fact in its role as learner. The traditional harmonization remained intact, but its rationale and *raison d'être* was now revolutionized.

It must, however, be stressed that the harmonization of knowledge is nowadays to be seen in fundamentally pragmatic terms. It is not a matter of discovery—of finding at the end of a long course of inquiry that we have discovered a harmonious reality. Instead, it is the other way round: The standard of acceptability that we ourselves endorse with respect to the distinction between conjecture and fact views the harmony of fact as a pivotal validating factor in our entitlement to claim certain contentions as true rather than merely problematic or conjectural. The reality is that our view of the factual domain is articulated with a view to its harmonious systematization because it is just here that cogency and intelligence can effectively come to grips with the materials we can rationally accept as affording us knowledge of the real.

Cognitive Systematicity as a Hallmark of the Scientific

The ideal of a harmonious systematicity of knowledge is often seen as the hallmark of science. As Kant for one insisted, it is their systematicity that in fact authenticates the claims of individual theses as actually belonging to a *science:* "As systematic unity is what first raises ordinary knowledge to the rank of science, that is, makes a system out of a mere aggregate of knowledge, architectonic [the art of constructing systems] is the doctrine of the scientific in our knowledge."[18]

Let us explore more extensively the contention—deeply rooted in the epistemological tradition of the West—that the proper, *scientific* development of our knowledge should proceed systematically. Scientific systematization has two aspects. The first is *methodological* and looks to the unity provided by common intellectual tools of inquiry and argumentation. (This aspect of the unity of a shared body of methodological machinery was the focus of the "Unity of Science" movement in the heyday of logical positivism in the 1920s and '30s.) But, of course, there should be a *substantive* unity as well. Something would be very seriously amiss if we could not bring the various sectors of science into coordination and consonance with one another. And even when there are or appear to be conflicts and discordances, we should be able to explain them and provide a rational account for them within an overarching framework of explanatory principles.

Scientific explanation in general proceeds along *subsumptive* lines, particular occurrences in nature being explained with reference to covering generalizations. But the *adequacy* of such an explanation hinges on the status of the covering generalization: is it a "mere empirical regularity," or is it a thesis whose standing within our scientific system is firmly secured as a "law of nature"? This latter question leads straightaway to the pivotal issue of how firmly the thesis is embedded within its wider systematic setting in the branch of science at issue. Systematization here affords a criterion of the appositeness of the generalizations deployed in scientific explanation.

An empirical generalization is not to be viewed as fully adequate for explanatory purposes until it can claim the status of a law. And a law is not just a summary statement of observed regularities to date; it claims to deal with a universal regularity purporting to describe how things inevitably are: how the processes at work in the world must invariably work, how things have to happen in nature. Such a claim has to be based on a stronger foundation than any mere observed regularity to date. The *coherence of laws* in patterns that illuminate the functional "mechanisms" by which natural processes occur is a critical element—perhaps the most pivotal one—in furnishing this stronger foundation, this "something more" than a mere generalization of observation. And "observed regularity" does not qualify for acceptance as a "law of nature" simply by becoming better established through observation in additional cases: what is required is *coordinative integration* into the body of scientific knowledge.[19]

Systematicity is thus not only a prominent (if partial) aspect of the structure of our knowledge, but is a normatively *desirable* aspect of it—indeed a *requisite* for genuinely scientific knowledge. It is, accordingly, correlative with the *regulative* ideal presented by the injunction: develop your knowledge so as to endow it with a systematic structure of reciprocal coordination. To understand an issue properly—that is, to understand it scientifically—we must grasp it in its systematic setting. *Sapientis est ordinare* affirms the sage dictum of which Thomas Aquinas was fond.[20] And so as he saw it their methodological role as instruments of scientific reasoning reflects—and makes manifest—the fundamentally regulative nature of the parameters of cognitive systematization (simplicity, uniformity, and so on). They combine to mark the endeavor to instill our knowledge of the world with the hallmarks of systems as a definitive feature of scientific inquiry. The parameters of systematicity accordingly emerge as prime tools of scientific method.

It is through the heritage of the Leibniz-Wolff-Kant tradition in particular that systematization has become for the moderns, too, an ongoing vehicle for the ancient ideal of a *scientia*—a body of knowledge developed as a comprehensive whole according to rational principles. And, indeed, the prospect of organizing a body of claims systematically is crucial to its claims to being a science. Systematization monitors the adequacy of the rational development (articulation) of what we claim to know, authenticating the whole body of claims, collectively, as a science. As Kant put it, "systematic unity is what first raises ordinary knowledge to the rank of science."[21]

There can be no science without system. Systematicity is the very hallmark of a science: a "science" is—virtually by definition—a branch of knowledge that systematizes our information in some domain of empirical fact. Accordingly, Kant espoused the schema: the science of X is the systematization of all of our attainable knowledge regarding X.[22] In a remarkably Hegelian vein, he wrote: "Systems seem to be formed . . . in the sheer self-development of reason. Hence, not only is each system articulated in accordance with an idea, but they are one and all organically united in a system of human knowledge, as members of one whole, and so as admitting of an architectonic of all human knowledge which at the present time, in view of the great amount of material that has been collected, or which can be obtained from the ruins of ancient systems, is not only possible, but would not indeed be difficult."[23] This idea of the systematically comprehensive self-development of reason is present in much of the subsequent philosophical tradition, particularly in the school of Hegel.

Prominent in the historical background here is Leibniz's bold vision of a *scientia universalis*—a synoptic treatment of all knowledge—encyclopedic in scope, yet ordered not by the customary, conventional, and arbitrary arrangement of letters of the alphabet, but a rational arrangement of topics according to their immanent cognitive principles. The conception of scientific systematization points toward the ideal of a perfect science within which all the available and relevant facts about the world occupy a suitable place with due regard to their cognitive connections. Indeed, not only should scientific knowledge approximate—and, ideally, *constitute*—one vast synoptic system, but a discipline is validated as authentically scientific by its inclusion within the overall system.

The search for cognitive system thus brings together our deepest intellectual and aesthetic aspirations. As Karl Pearson put it long ago,

There is an insatiable desire in the human breast to resume in some short formula, some brief statement, the facts of human experience. It leads the savage to "account" for all natural phenomena by deifying the wind and the stream and the tree. It leads civilised man, on the other hand, to express his emotional experience in works of art, and his physical and mental experience in the formulae or so-called laws of science. . . . Science endeavors to provide a mental *résumé* of the universe, and its last great claim to our support is the capacity it has for satisfying our cravings for a brief description of the history of the world. Such a brief description, a formula resuming all things, science has not yet found and may probably never find, but of this we may feel sure, that its method of seeking for one is the sole possible method, and that the truth it has reached is the only form of truth which can permanently satisfy the aesthetic judgment.[24]

The drive for system represents a synthesis of the cognitive and aesthetic domains of the human intellect to which no creative scientist is wholly insensitive in this thought. (Recall Rosalind Franklin's remark that the Watson-Crick double-helix model "is just too pretty to be wrong.")

And the idea of harmony runs parallel with the systematization. As is to be expected, here, too, matters begin with the Greeks of classical antiquity. Aristotle tells us that the Pythagoreans taught that numbers are the elements of all things and that the whole universe is constituted as a harmony of numbers (Aristotle, *Metaphysics*, 986a 2–8). Moreover, they held that love, virtue, health, and everything positive in nature is constituted as a harmony (*kath' harmonian synestanai ta hola: Diogenes Laertius*, VIII, 33).

According to Heraclitus conflicting opposites harmonize in constituting the natural world[25]—an idea later developed by Nicholas of Cusa in his doctrine of the unity of opposites (*coincidentia oppositorum*) and by Giordano Bruno. However, the philosopher of harmony par excellence was G. W. Leibniz. For him the world was established in principles of harmony, and natural reality is as harmonious an existential manifold as it is possible to realize: "There is nothing in the world of created beings whose perfected conception does not involve the conception of every other thing in the universe, since each thing influences all the others in such a way that, supposing that it were abandoned or changed, all things in the world would henceforward be different from the way they actually are."[26] Prizing the harmony of systems is a philosophical stance that is virtually as old as the subject itself.

The Hegelian Inversion: From a Desideratum of Exposition to a Test of Acceptability

An important development in this range of ideas came with Hegel and his followers in the nineteenth century. This was the transformation from the earlier conception of systematicity as the hallmark of science, as per the equation

a science = a systematically developed body of knowledge,

into its redeployment as a criterion or standard of cognitive acceptability, as per the equation

true (presumptively) = meriting inclusion within a science = capable of being smoothly integrated into the system of scientific knowledge.

We thus arrive at the "Hegelian inversion" by beginning with the implication thesis that what belongs to science can be systematized and then transposing it into the converse:

If an item is systematizable with the whole of our (purported) knowledge, then it should be accepted as a part of it.

Systematicity is now set up as a testing standard of (presumptive) truth and thus becomes a means for enlarging the realm of what we accept as true, rather than merely affording a device for organizing preestablished truth.

The earlier discussions stressed the overall systematicity of "the truth"—the fact that the totality of true theses must constitute a cohesive system—and presented system as a crucial aspect of truth. This pre-Hegelian approach saw systematization as a two-step process: first determine truths and then systematize them. (Think of the analogy of building a wall: first the bricks are assembled and then the wall is built.) With the inversion at issue, a single-step process emerges: the determination of the right components through the very process of their being assembled.

This line of development points to a characteristic and distinctive and importantly different role for systematicity, for its bearing is now radically transformed. From being a hallmark *of science* (according to the regulative idea that a body of knowledge claims cannot qualify as a science if it lacks a systematic articulation), the harmonization of information is transmuted into *a standard of truth*, an acceptability criterion for the claims that purport to belong to science. From a *desideratum of the organization* of our "body of factual knowledge," systematicity is metamorphosed into a *qualifying test of membership* in it—a standard of facticity. The effect of the Hegelian inversion is to establish "the claim of system as an arbiter of fact," to use F. H. Bradley's apt expression.

This idea of systematicity as an arbiter of knowledge was implicit in Hegel himself, and developed by his followers, particularly those of the English Hegelian school inaugurated by T. H. Green. This Hegelian inversion leads to one of the central themes of the present discussion—the idea of using systematization as a control of substantive knowledge. Bradley put the matter this way: "The test [of truth] which I advocate is the idea of a whole of knowledge as wide and as consistent as may be. In speaking of system I as the standard [of truth] I always mean the union of these two aspects [of coherence and comprehensiveness] . . . [which] are for me inseparably included in the idea of system. . . . Facts for it [that is, my view] are true . . . just so far as they contribute to the order of experience. If by taking certain judgments . . . as true, I can get some system into my world, then these 'facts' are so far true, and if by taking certain 'facts' as errors I can order my experience better, then these 'facts' are errors."[27]

The plausibility of such an approach is easy to see. Pilate's question is still relevant. How are we humans—imperfect mortals dwelling in this imperfect sublunary sphere—to determine where "the real truth" lies? The Recording Angel does not whisper it into our ears. (If he did, I doubt that we would understand him!) The consideration that we have no direct access to the truth regarding the modus operandi of the world we inhabit is perhaps the most fundamental fact of epistemology. We must recognize that there is no prospect of assessing the truth—or presumptive truth—of claims in this domain independently of our efforts at systematization in scientific inquiry. The Hegelian idea of truth assessment through systematization represents a hard-headed and inherently attractive effort to adjust and accommodate to this fundamental fact.

To see more vividly some of the philosophical ramifications of this Hegelian approach, let us glance back once more to the epistemological role of systematicity in its historical aspect. The point of departure was the Greek position (encountered in Plato and Aristotle and clearly operative still with rationalists as late as Spinoza) that—secure in a fundamental commitment to the systematicity of the real—took cognitive systematicity (that is, systematicity as present in the framework of "our knowledge") as a measure of the extent to which our purported understanding of the world can be regarded as adequate via the principle of *adaequatio ad rem*. Here, systematicity functions as a *regulative ideal for the organization of knowledge* and (accordingly) as a standard for the *organizational adequacy* of our cognitive claims. But the approach of the Hegelian school (and the Academic Skeptics of classical antiquity who had anticipated them in this regard) moves well beyond this position. Viewing systematicity not merely as a *regulative* ideal for knowledge but as an epistemically constitutive principle, it extends what was a mere test of understanding into a test of the evidential acceptability of factual truth claims. Explanatory systematicity comes to operate as evidential warrant.

Accordingly, the Hegelian inversion sees the transformation of systematicity from a framework for organizing knowledge into a mechanism for characterizing adequate knowledge claims. Fit, attunement, and systematic connection become the criteria with which to determine the acceptability of knowledge claims. With this approach, our "picture of the real" emerges as an intellectual product achieved under the control of the ideal of system as a regulative principle for our theorizing.

Metaphysical Ramifications of the Hegelian Inversion

Interesting metaphysical implications for the bearing of systemic harmony on the interrelation between truth and reality emerge from this perspective. Let us approach the issue in its historical dimension. A line of thought pervasively operative since antiquity may be set out by the syllogism:

REALITY IS A COHERENT SYSTEM.
KNOWLEDGE AGREES WITH REALITY.

KNOWLEDGE IS A COHERENT SYSTEM.

With Kant's Copernican revolution this traditional mode of appeal to the classical conception of truth *adaequatio intellectu ad rem* came to be transformed to:

KNOWLEDGE IS A COHERENT SYSTEM.
KNOWLEDGE AGREES WITH (EMPIRICAL) REALITY.

REALITY (THAT IS, EMPIRICAL REALITY) IS A COHERENT SYSTEM.

While the original syllogism effectively bases a conclusion about knowledge on premises regarding reality, its Kantian transformation bases a conclusion about reality on premises regarding knowledge. In the wake of Kant's Copernican revolution, the ontological emphasis becomes dependent and derivative, seeing that our only available pathway to reality itself leads through our reality: our cognitive endeavors to form pictures of the real.

With this aspect of Kant's Copernican revolution we reach the idea that in espousing the dictum "truth is a system," what one is actually claiming to be systematic is not the world as such but our knowledge of it. Accordingly, it is what is known to be true regarding "the facts" of nature that is systematized, and systematicity thus becomes, in the first instance, a feature of knowledge rather than of its subject matter.

The idea of system can—indeed, must—be applied by us to nature, yet not to nature in itself and *an sich*, but rather to "nature insofar as nature conforms to our power of judgment."[28] Correspondingly, system is at bottom not a constitutive conception descriptive of reality per se, but a regulative conception descriptive of how our thought regarding reality must proceed.

Kant's successors wanted to "overcome" his residual allegiance to the Cartesian divide between our knowledge and its object. Carrying the motto "The real is rational" on their banners, they sought to restore system to its Greek position as a fundamentally ontological— rather than merely epistemological—concept. In this setting, however, the concept of the systematization of truth played the part of a controlling ideal more emphatically than ever.

Hegel, in effect, was led back to the Greeks by asking in Kantian style: How do we really know that knowledge is a coherent system? But he was discontented with Kant's setting up as a major premise what for him (and the Greeks) ought to have been a conclusion. And so he answered the question in a very different way. Here is the key principle of the Hegelian inversion he used as his starting point:

> If a thesis coheres systematically with the rest of what is known, then—and only then—is it a part of real knowledge (which accordingly characterizes reality itself).

Now, it is clear that once we adopt this principle as our operative defining standard (criterion, arbiter) of knowledge—so that only what is validated in terms of this coherentist principle is admitted into "our knowledge"—then the crucial contention that "knowledge is a coherent system" at once follows and so returns to the status of a conclusion rather than a premise. If, as is only sensible, the epistemic constituting of our (purported) knowledge takes place in terms of considerations of systematic coherence, then it follows—now without any reference to directly ontological considerations—that the body of knowledge so constituted will have to form a coherent system. (But in here taking such an epistemic rather than an ontological route we Hegelians, too, reveal ourselves as true children of the era inaugurated by Kant's Copernican revolution.)[29]

The previous deliberations have offered a three-part answer to the question, "What is the point of cognitive systematization?"

1. Systematization provides a vehicle for making claims *intelligible*.
2. Systematization authenticates a body of knowledge as developed scientifically: it is a test of the *scientific adequacy* for expositions of knowledge.
3. In providing quality control at the wholesale level of a body of knowledge, systematicity also provides a means for testing purported knowledge claims for inclusion in our "body of knowledge." It thus affords a probative instrument, *a test of acceptability* (or correctness) for factual claims.

And to these three fundamental points, the Hegelian Inversion adds yet another:

4. Systematization provides the definitive constituting criterion of knowledge: it is the operative mechanism for authenticating knowledge as such.[30]

Whereas thesis (3) comes to a test standard "if adequately systematized, then presumably true," thesis (4) comes to the very different "if *fully and perfectly* systematized, then *certainly true*." In these varying yet related ways, systemic harmony comes to serve a crucial role in the quality control of knowledge in the factual domain. For we would not and could not reasonably accept an item of knowledge as such if it did not harmonize with the rest.

British and American neo-Hegelians above all stressed the idea that the world's facts have to fit together into a harmonious whole. As Brand Blanshard says with reference to Bradley, "But they [the Idealist coherence theorists] did in general follow him [Bradley] in holding that the real was coherent in a double sense, first in being consistent throughout in spite of apparent incongruities, secondly in being interdependent throughout, that is, so ordered that every fact was connected necessarily with the others and ultimately with all."[31] The truth, the idealists held, must constitute a rational system of knowledge in which every statement is inseparably interconnected with the rest. As H. H. Joachim puts it, "a system possesses self-coherence (a) in proportion as every constituent element of it logically involves and is involved by every other; and (b) in so far as the reciprocal implications of the constituent elements, or rather the constituent elements in their reciprocal implications, constitute alone and completely the significance of the system"[32]

The systematic harmonization to knowledge is a powerfully attractive ideal.[33] For any rent in the fabric of our scientific knowledge— any failings in point of its unity and orderliness—would clearly deserve to be characterized as a flaw, and would be seen as an impediment to the adequacy of our understanding and the effectiveness of our intellectual mastery. To be sure, no one claims that such synoptic and comprehensive systematization is a descriptive aspect of scientific knowledge as it stands today (or will stand at some other historical juncture). But it represents an idealization toward which—by widespread agreement—science can and should progress along an evolutionary route. And this grandiose and heroic vision that all of our knowledge of our environing universe forms part of a single harmonious, all-embracing cognitive system is one of the great formative ideas of Western civilization.

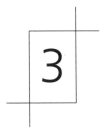

3

The Systematicity of Nature
Harmonia Mundi

Cognitive and Ontological Systematicity

Throughout the history of philosophy, the idea of the world as a structured system of harmoniously coordinated processes has figured among the mainstream ideas of Western thought.[1] And the conception of a harmonious system has historically been applied both to *the world's makeup* and to *bodies of knowledge,* so that the harmony of cognitive systematization stands alongside the harmony of nature itself. Now, to all appearances the systematization of our knowledge about the natural world has roots in the fact that nature itself is a harmonious manifold of processes so that *cognitive* systematicity of our (putative) knowledge or *information* about things parallels the *ontological* systematicity (simplicity, coherence, regularity, uniformity) of the *objects* of our knowledge—that is, systematicity as a feature of things. In fact, three significantly distinguishable roles must be assigned to systematicity:

I. Cognitive Systematicity

1. *Codificational systematicity*: systematicity as a feature of the organization of our knowledge.
2. *Criterial systematicity*: systematicity as a criterial test standard for assessing the acceptability of theses.

II. Ontological Systematicity

3. *Ontological systematicity:* systematicity as a descriptive characteristic of objects—including, in principle, that of the whole of
   the natural universe, the *harmonia mundi.*

Given such a distinction of several modes of systematicity, there arises
the priority question of their relative fundamentality. In particular we
must ask: where does primacy lie—is systemic harmony essentially an
epistemic desideratum for our knowledge regarding nature or an ontologically descriptive feature of nature itself?

Procedural or Methodological Systematicity

From the epistemic standpoint, the parameters of systemic harmony—simplicity, coherence, regularity, and so on—can effectively
serve to regulate and control the claims of our explanatory-descrip-
tive accounts of the world to rational acceptability. In particular, they
can serve as *regulative principles of inquiry,* as instruments for assessing appropriateness and acceptability in the conduct of our cognitive
endeavors. If a characterization of the workings of nature manifested
a substantial lack of cognitive systematization, then it would thereby
betoken its own inadequacy. One could not rationally rest content
with such an account because, by hypothesis, it contravenes what is in
fact a characterizing condition of an *adequate* account. But this perspective on cognitive systematicity is not the whole of the story.

In the days of the medieval Schoolmen and of those later ratio-
nalistic philosophers whom Kant was wont to characterize as dogma-
tists, simplicity was viewed as an *ontological feature of the world.* Just
as it was then held that "Nature abhors a vacuum"—and, perhaps
more plausibly, "In nature there is an explanation for everything"—
so it was contended that "Nature abhors complexity." Kant's Copernican revolution shifted the responsibility for such desiderata from
physical nature to the human intellect. Simplicity-tropism accordingly became not a feature of "the real world" but rather one of "the mechanisms of human thought" (though perhaps one that is " hardwired"
into the human intellect). Kant acutely observed that what was at issue

was a facet not of the teleology of *nature* but of the teleology of *reason*, responsibility for which lay not with the theory but with the theorizers. The subsequent Darwinian revolution took this process a step further. It removed the teleological element. Neither nature nor human rational faculties were now seen as an ontological locus of systematicity-preference, but its rationale was placed on a *strictly methodological* basis. And there is much justice in this position. For in the end responsibility for systematicity-tropism lies not with the "hardware" of human reason but with its "software"—that is, with the methodological principles that we ourselves employ because we find systematically articulated theories easier to work with and more effective.

On such a perspective, then, our systematicity-based inductive practices are seen as a fundamentally regulative and procedural resource in the domain of inquiry, proceeding in implementation of the injunction "Do all you reasonably can to enhance the extent to which your cognitive commitments are simple, cohesive, and smoothly systematic."

The crucial point is that acquiring and managing information is a purposive human activity—like most of our endeavors. And as such it involves the ongoing expenditure of resources for the realization of the objectives—description, explanation, prediction, and control—that represent the defining characteristics of our cognitive endeavors. The balance of costs and benefits becomes critical here and endows the cognitive enterprise with an unavoidably economic aspect. The value of systematicity with its consistent features of coherence, simplicity, and so on is something that is inherent in the rationally mandated modus operandi of a creature that must make optimal use of limited cognitive resources.

The Regulative/Methodological Character
of Cognitive Systematicity

It is important, however, to distinguish economy of means from economy of product—procedural from substantive economy. Simple tools or methods can, suitably used, create complicated results. A simple cognitive method, such as trial and error, can ultimately yield complex answers to difficult questions. Conversely, simple results are sometimes brought about in convoluted ways. A complicated method of inquiry or problem solving might yield easy and uncomplicated solutions. Our commitment to simplicity in scientific inquiry does not, in the end, prevent us from discovering whatever complexities are actually there. The role of chance, chaos, and complexity *as aspects of reality itself* cannot be ruled out. Since the bearing of *cognitive* systematicity is *regulative* rather than *descriptive* in orientation, it is altogether lacking in substantive and ontological involvements, for in the final analysis it is not that nature avoids complexity but that *we* do so—insofar as we find it possible.

Induction is no more than a search for cognitive order in the resolution of our questions, and our processes of inductive inquiry into nature are geared to reveal orderliness *if it is there.* When fishing, a net whose mesh has a certain area will catch fish of a certain size *if* any are present. Use of the net indicates a *hope,* perhaps even an *expectation* that the fish will be there, but certainly not a pressured *foreknowledge* of their presence. Nothing in the abstract logic of the situation guarantees a priori that we shall find order when we go looking for it in the world. (Our cognitive search for order and system may issue in a finding of disorder and chaos.) Whether the world is such that systematic knowledge of it is possible is an ultimately *contingent* question whose answer must itself emerge from our actual endeavors at systematization.

The parameters of cognitive systematicity—simplicity, regularity, coherence, conformity, and the rest—generally represent principles of economy of operation. They implement the idea of epistemic preferability or precedence, of presumption and burden of proof, by indicating where, in the absence of specific counterindications, our epistemic commitments are to be placed in weaving the fabric of our knowledge. In this way they are labor-saving devices for avoiding complications in the conduct of our cognitive business. Such a procedural/ methodological mechanism does not prejudge or preempt any ultimate substantive finding, but it does decisively guide and control the process by which the answer—whatever it may be—is attained.

To be sure, only time will eventually tell the extent to which we can successfully move in the direction that systematicity and its concomitant factors of elegance, such as simplicity and coherence, point us with respect to our scientific knowledge of the world. This is something that "remains to be seen." (And here the importance of ultimate experiential retrovalidation comes in to supplement our commitment to methodological convenience.) But these factors clearly afford the most natural and promising starting point. The systematically smoothest resolution of our questions is patently that which must be allowed to prevail—at any rate *pro tem,* until such time as its untenability becomes manifest. Where a simple solution will accommodate the data at hand, there is no good reason for turning elsewhere.

Accordingly, one need not prejudge that the world *is* a system in order to set about the enterprise of striving to know it systematically. The finding of ontological systematicity (orderliness, lawfulness) in nature—to whatever extent that nature indeed *is* systematic—is a substantive product of systematizing inquiry, rather than a needed input or presupposition for it. For it is a regulative or action-guiding *presumption* and not a constitutive or world-descriptive *principle* that is at issue—in the first instance at any rate.[2] We are to *proceed as though* nature in fact exhibited those modes of systematicity needed for systematizing inquiry to bear fruit. Its confirmation, as in requisite degree present as a matter of descriptive fact at the *substantive* level, is something that must come later on, in the course of inquiry rather than at its outset.

But does not the prospect that its objective may well be unattainable impede the appropriateness of adopting simplicity as an ideal of inquiry? Surely not. The validation of this cognitive ideal does *not* lie in the fact that its realization can be guaranteed a priori from the outset. We may in fact never realize it. But this possibility should not be allowed to impede our efforts to press the project of systematization as far as we possibly can. Here, as elsewhere, the validity of an ideal does not call for any prior guarantee of its ultimate realization. (What ideal is ever validated in this way?) To be sure, a hope of its eventual realization can never in principle be finally and totally demolished. But this feeble comfort is hardly sufficient to establish its propriety.

The long and short of it is that while we have no a priori assurance of ultimate success in the quest for systematicity, a standing presumption in favor of this key cognitive ideal is nevertheless rationally legitimate because of its furtherance of the inherent aims and objective of the cognitive enterprise. In sum, the validation of systematicity as a cognitive ideal roots in essentially practical consideration of its proven utility. However, as we pursue this line of thought, further important aspects of the relationship between the world's cognitive and ontological systematicity also come to light, namely, those relating to its regulative role.

On Cognitive and Substantive Systematicity

Cognitive systematicity characterizes the procedural structure of our endeavors to *organize* our knowledge of the world. It embodies methodological or regulative principles of epistemic plausibility and presumption—principles in the sense of rules governing how we are to proceed in the conduct of our cognitive affairs, and not principles in the sense of theses describing how things work in the world. There is no question here of presupposing the ontological systematicity of nature. A regulative presumption of the sort at issue here is a rule of cognitive procedure or of method, not an assumption of fact.

Systematicity seeking thus emerges as a salient aspect of the rational methodology of inquiry in general and philosophical inquiry in particular. But such a methodology seeks to reveal orderliness *if it is there*. In the final analysis the fact that the natural world is indeed a harmonious system is a statement about its nature and not merely an artifact of the methods we employ in investigating it.

How is it that we know the world to be a cohesively harmonious system? Charles Sanders Peirce wrote: "Underlying all such principles [of cognitive methodology] there is a fundamental and primary . . . hypothesis which we must embrace at the outset, however destitute of evidentiary support it may be [at this stage]. That hypothesis is that the facts in hand admit of rationalization, and rationalization by us. That we must hope they do, for the same reason that a general who has to capture a position or see his country ruined, must go on the hypothesis that there is some way in which he can and shall capture it. We must be animated by that hope concerning the problem we have in hand."[3] This passage almost gets the matter straight—almost, but not quite. To be sure, in philosophy we must "act as though" the hypothesis were correct; we must, as was said, effectively deploy this particular as-if as a regulative presumption that serves us as a *principle of procedure* in this cognitive domain. But it is not necessary (save perhaps for psychological reasons of morale) for us to *embrace* this hypothesis—we need not assume or postulate it. Initially there need be no actual credence at all, and one can proceed in an experimental spirit, by the provisional adoption of a *mere* hypothesis. (One can assume the stance of the injunction: "*Allez en avant et la foi vous viendra.*") A methodologically motivated *presumption* in favor of ontological systematicity accordingly does not involve us in any vicious or vitiating circularity. It is a regulative or action-guiding *practical presumption* that governs our philosophical praxis and not a constitutive or world-descriptive *principle* that is at issue—in the first instance at any rate. On this basis we are to proceed until further notice as though nature in fact exhibited those modes of systematicity needed for systematizing inquiry to bear fruit. Its legitimation is a matter of descriptive fact at the *substantive* level, something that must—and, indeed, does—come later on, as a product rather than a presupposition.

Cognitive systematicity remains an epistemic factor that does not of itself prejudice our findings regarding the nature of reality. Its reason for being lies with those who conduct the inquiry and not with the descriptive character of objects at which the inquiry aims. In this approach, the parameters of systematicity serve as *regulative principles of inquiry:* instruments for assessing intelligibility and acceptability in managing our philosophical endeavors.

If a philosophical characterization of putative facts were in substantial violation of these regulative desiderata of cognitive systematization, then it would thereby blazon forth its own inadequacy. One could not rationally rest content with such an account because—by hypothesis—it contravenes what is in fact one of the very characterizing conditions of an *adequate* account. The manifold of what we see as putative fact—considered as a distinct cognitive structure in its own right—should ideally leave no room for chance, absurdity, or the haphazard. But the role of the surd *as an aspect of reality itself* cannot be negated a priori. In its critical role, the bearing of *cognitive* systematicity is thus seen to be *regulative* rather than *descriptive* in orientation and, accordingly, as lacking in substantive commitments and ontological involvements. No substantive prejudgments in relation to the world's harmonious systematicity are being made in philosophy on the basis of this methodological approach.

But at this point it must be reemphasized that the systemic harmony of science has two aspects: process (scientific method and investigative methodology) and product (the ultimate world picture that our scientific inquiries provide). Process is a matter of theoretical general principles along the lines of philosophical reflection as set out in our preceding deliberations. Now, product is there as well. However, it is something quite different—a feature of the real that emerges not from the general principles of philosophical deliberations but from the substantive findings that ensue from the empirical investigation of nature and its ways.

Cognitive Systematicity as an Indicator of Ontological Systematicity

Ontological systematicity relates to the orderliness and lawfulness of nature—to its conformity to *rules* and *principles* of various sorts. Now, if nature were not rulish in exhibiting manifold regularities—if it were pervasively "unruly" (say, because its laws changed rapidly and randomly)—then anything approaching a scientific study of the world would clearly be impossible. The modes of orderliness at issue in the various parameters of systematicity (simplicity, regularity, coherence, uniformity, consistency, and the rest) are all related to aspects of the workings of nature that underpin the possibility of scientific inquiry.

If natural science is to be possible at all, then our situation in nature must be such that our local environment is sufficiently systematic (orderly, regular) to permit the orderly conduct of rational inquiry, and thus, a fortiori, the existence of intelligent beings capable of it. If the world were not orderly (both in itself and as concerns the modus operandi of inquiring creatures), then there would be no uniformity in information gathering, information storage, and so on, and consequently there would be no avenue to the acquisition of knowledge of the world—or, indeed, even putative knowledge of it. If the attainment—nay, even the pursuit—of knowledge is to be possible for us, the world must be at any rate sufficiently orderly to permit our cognitive functioning. This rulishness is basic to the very possibility of natural science. The aims of science—the description, explanation, prediction, and control of nature—would clearly be altogether unrealizable in a world that is sufficiently badly asystematic. A significant degree of ontological systematicity *in* the world is (obviously) a causal requisite for realizing codificational systematicity in our knowledge *of* the world. Thus, while the ontological systematicity of the world is not a *conceptual presupposition* for the success of systematizing inquiry, it is nevertheless—at least in some degree—a *causal precondition* for this success. A world that is insufficiently systematic and verges on chaos cannot provide an environment within which inductive learning is possible. (To be sure, a world that admits of knowledge acquisition need not be a *total* system; *partial* systematicity will do: merely enough to permit orderly inquiry in our cosmic neighborhood by beings constituted as we are.)

And so, while our commitment to inductive systematicity is initially a matter of methodological convenience within the overall economy of rational procedure, nevertheless, it is in the final event not totally devoid of ontological commitments regarding the world's nature. To be sure, things need not *be* systematic to admit of systematic study and discussion: the systematicity of the real is not a prerequisite for systematicity in knowledge of it. (Knowledge need not share the features of its objects: to speak of a sober study of inebriation or a dispassionate analysis of passions is not a contradiction in terms.) However, while its converse fails, as we have seen, the implication that

$$(X \text{ is ontologically systematic}) \rightarrow \begin{bmatrix} \text{information about } X \text{ is} \\ \text{in principle cognitively} \\ \text{systematizable} \end{bmatrix}$$

is nevertheless a necessary one. Ontological systematicity is in fact a sufficient condition for cognitive systematizability. For clearly such implications as the following will hold:

> If no simple *account* of a thing is in principle realizable, then it cannot itself be simple, ontologically speaking.
>
> If no coherent *explanation* of a process is in principle realizable, then it cannot itself be coherent, ontologically speaking.
>
> If no uniform *description* of a thing is in principle realizable, then it cannot itself be uniform, ontologically speaking.

The parameters of systematicity are accordingly such that the following basic principle holds:

> If a thing *is* itself ontologically simple (uniform, coherent), then a simple (uniform, coherent) *account* of it must in principle be possible (however difficult we may find its realization in practice).

Thus, while cognitive systematicity cannot provide deductively necessitating evidence for ontological systematicity, nevertheless it certainly provides an *inductive* indication of ontological systematicity. And, in fact, cognitive systematicity of a suitable kind affords the *best*—perhaps the *only*—empirical evidence we can ever actually obtain on behalf of ontological systematicity; the former constitutes the best available criterion or evidential indicator of the latter.

The Ontological Ramifications of Simplicity

But the aim of inquiry is to get at the truth of things, and is there any reason to think that simpler theories have a better prospect of being true? Clearly, there are difficulties here. Does nature exhibit a penchant for simplicity? Surely not. We cannot say, solely on the basis of general principles of some sort, that this world—the real world as such—must of necessity be a simple one. Nor is there any real need for doing so.

An eminent philosopher has written: "Actually in cases of inductive simplicity it is not economy which determines our choice. . . . We make the assumption that the simplest theory furnishes the best predictions. This assumption cannot be justified by convenience: it has a truth character and demands a justification within the theory of probability and induction."[4] This perspective is gravely misleading. What sort of consideration would possibly justify the supposition that "the simplest theory furnishes the best predictions"? Any such belief is surely inappropriate. Induction with respect to the history of science itself—a constant series of errors of oversimplification—would soon undermine our confidence that nature operates in the way we would deem the simplest. On the contrary, the history of science is a highly repetitive story of simple theories giving way to more complicated and sophisticated ones. The Greeks had four elements; in the nineteenth century, Mendeleev had some eighty; we nowadays have a vast series of stability states. Aristotle's cosmos had only spheres; Ptolemy's added epicycles; ours has a virtually endless proliferation of complex orbits that only supercomputers can approximate. Greek science could be transmitted on a shelf of books; that of the Newtonian age required a roomful; ours requires vast storage structures filled not only with books and journals but with photographs, tapes, floppy disks, and so on. Of the quantities nowadays recognized as the fundamental constants of physics, only one was contemplated in Newton's physics, the universal gravitational constant; a second was added in the nineteenth century, Avogadro's constant. The remaining six are all creatures of twentieth-century physics: the speed of light (the velocity of electromagnetic radiation in free space), the elementary charge, the rest mass of the electron, the rest mass of the proton, Planck's constant, and Boltzmann's constant.[5] It would be naive—and quite wrong—to think that the course of scientific progress is one of increasing simplicity.

A methodologically based approach to the rationalization of inductive systematicity on grounds of economy accordingly is not predicated on presupposing any sort of ontological linkage between simplicity and (probable) truth. In the first instance, at any rate, the thesis that nature is a system is a merely regulative principle, a guideline of epistemic procedure or policy. The basis of simplicity preference is thus methodological or epistemological rather than substantive or ontological.[6] The pivotal role that science assigns to cognitive virtues like simplicity, coherence, systematicity, fecundity, symmetry, and generality on first view appears as problematic and question begging. It is only when we turn to the methodological standpoint of procedural economy that everything falls easily and naturally into place.

It is important, however, to distinguish economy of means from economy of product—methodological from material economy. Simple tools or methods can, suitably used, create complicated results. A simple cognitive method, such as trial and error, can ultimately yield complex answers to difficult questions. Conversely, simple results are sometimes brought about in complicated ways. A complicated method of inquiry or problem solving might yield easy and uncomplicated problem solutions. Our commitment to simplicity in scientific inquiry does not, in the end, prevent us from discovering whatever complexities are actually there.

To be sure, this methodological/procedural tale is not the whole story. There is also, in the final analysis, a substantive aspect to the matter of induction's justification. Our intellectual tastes (for simplicity, elegance, and so on, as we naturally construe these ideas) are, like our physical tastes (palatability), the product of evolutionary pressure to prioritize those things that work—that prove effective and are thus survival conducive. The evolutionary aspect of our cognitive mechanisms assures the serviceability of the cognitive values we standardly invoke as effective conditions of adequacy for the substantiation of information. The presence of positive values in information enhances the utility of that information, not because nature is benign or because a preestablished harmony is at work, but because evolution—both biological and cultural—so operates as to assure alignment. Nature exacts its penalties for ineffectiveness, and evolutionary pressure toward cost effectiveness assures an inherent connection between functional adequacy and temporal survival. The evolutionary realities assure an important role for economic considerations in the theory of knowledge. There is a tight linkage between a cognitively advantageous economy of intellectual effort and a biologically advantageous economy of physical effort.

Take memory, for example. In general, the information we most urgently need is just the information that we most frequently use. And repeated use renders it familiar, impressing it more deeply into our memory with each repetition. The transit from need to use to familiarization to availability is assured by a convenient chain of statistical linkages that reflects the modus operandi of our memory. Evolution has so arranged matters that the recentness of our experience is significant for short-term memory and its frequency for long-term memory. As this example indicates, cost effectiveness is inevitably coordinated with the implicit rationality of evolutionary process by virtue of the survival conduciveness of arrangements that represent efficient ways of using limited resources.

Moreover, the development of our cognitive methods through rational selection also plays a key role in this connection. The process of cognitive evolution so unfolds as to assure the coordination of convenience with effectiveness, for a process of rational selection is at work to support the retention, promulgation, and transmission of those cognitive resources that prove themselves effective in operation. The burden of this evolutionary argument is not biological survival. The point is not that in a niche rivalry between Austere Simplifiers and Byzantine Complicators the former will eventually displace the latter biologically, but rather that, if both are intelligently persistent, the former will eventually outdistance the latter epistemologically, simply through the circumstance that they perform in more cost-efficient ways. In a community of intelligent and rational agents, cultural perpetuation and not biological selection alone will play a crucial part in the development of our cognitive instrumentalities.

Accordingly, our reliance on inductive systematicity is not wholly methodological but also has an ontological, realistic aspect, in that we learn by experience how to practice induction—that is, how to go about the process of a conservation of effort. Trial and error—that is, the course of experience—constrains us to bring methodological/procedural economy into alignment with substantive/ontological economy in our cognitive operations. In particular, the reification of the mechanisms of our simplest explanations (unobservable entities and the like) affords a powerful heuristic. It is the (empirically confined) efficacy of such a process that provides the ultimate justification of such a realistic approach. We are well advised to accept unobservable entities not because their existence is somehow confirmable in observation (which *ex hypothesi* it is not) but because experience shows that a methodology of inquiry predicated on such a simplifying assumption in the end affords our most efficient and effective resource.

Initially, the justification for relying on simplicity in the pursuit of our cognitive affairs will rest on an essentially instrumental basis. We at first prefer the optimally systematic (simple, uniform) alternative, because this is the most economical, the most convenient, thing to do. But we persist in this course because experience shows that using such economical methods is efficient, is optimally cost effective (relative to available alternatives) for the realization of the task. The regulative principles and procedures at issue in our inductive practices are ones whose legitimation lies in their being pragmatically retrovalidated through a demonstrated capacity to guide inquiry into successful channels.

Induction thus emerges as a matter of the pursuit of systemic economy in the cognitive sphere. Inductive simplicity and systematicity inhere in a regulative ideal of inquiry correlative with the procedural injunction. So organize your knowledge as to impart to it as much systematic structure as you possibly can! A cognitive venture based on the quest for simplicity and systematicity, while at first merely hopeful, is ultimately retrovalidated in experience by the fact that its pursuit enables us to realize the fundamental aims and purposes of the cognitive enterprise more efficiently than the available alternatives. Initially, the pivotal issue is simply the matter of our convenience in doing what must be done to serve our purposes. The whole ontological question of the systematicity of nature can safely be left to await the results of actual use of inductive processes. No prior presuppositions are needed in this regard.

Such a process of what might be characterized as *experiential retrojustification* underwrites, with ex post facto hindsight, the substantive conclusion that a methodology of inquiry geared to systematicity preference is efficient—that it accomplishes the ends at issue in the cognitive enterprise with due economy of means. For the pivotal fact is not that (as Reichenbach puts it) "we make the assumption that the simplest theory furnishes the best predictions"—an assumption obviously ill-advised in the light of experience—but that plausible expectation preindicates and actual experience retrojustifies the supposition that a process of inquiry that proceeds on this basis is comparatively efficient in the realization of our cognitive goals. The point is not that the simplest alternative demonstrably affords (or is more likely to afford) successful predictions of and interventions in nature, but that a policy of inquiry that embodies simplicity preference emerges as a relatively effective epistemological policy. In the end, our inductive preference for simplicity and systematicity finds its final justification in the fact that it affords an effective search policy for serviceable truth estimates regarding answers to our questions; it is a productive strategy of inquiry rather than an immediate index of truth.

The crux is that we ultimately learn by experience (and thus through inductive reasoning itself) how to accomplish our inductive business more effectively. Our recourse to induction—that is, that we should proceed by its means—is justified instrumentally. For induction is a self-improving process. Experience can itself teach us which ways of interpreting the fundamental procedural ideas of inductive practice (simplicity, conformity, generality, and the rest) can lead to improved performance in the transaction of our inductive business. By a cyclic feedback process of variation and trial and error, we learn to do induction more effectively. Economy and convenience play the crucial pioneering roles in initially justifying our practice of inductive systematization on procedural and methodological grounds. But, in their turn, the issues of effectiveness and success come to predominate at the subsequent stage of retrospective revalidation ex post facto. And the question of the seemingly preestablished harmony coordinating these two theoretically disparate factors of convenience and effectiveness is ultimately resolved on the basis of evolutionary considerations in the order of rational selection.[7]

And, therefore, while our commitment to the harmonization of inductive systematicity should be explained as a matter of methodological convenience within the overall economy of rational procedure, nevertheless, our reliance on simplicity is in the final analysis not totally devoid of ontological commitments regarding the world's nature, for our wisdom-of-hindsight experience with induction also enters into its overall justification and, indeed, crucially determines not *that* but *how* we perform inductions. And in this regard inductive systematization is at once both the method and the product of our actual course of experience in the harmonization at issue in thought-world coordination.

To be sure, the following objection might well be offered at this stage:

> Might there not be a theory that, in its makeup as a theory, is extremely complex, but according to which the modus operandi of nature itself is extremely simple?

But despite its surface plausibility this objection rests on a mistake. For nature cannot be simple (and so on) if our mental processes are not, seeing that we ourselves are a *part* of nature. If our intellectual dealings are not simple (or regular or generally systematic), then nature itself does not pervasively exhibit this characteristic either. The fact that our mental operations must be inserted into the world as a smoothly functioning integral part thereof means that a nature that incorporates such complex processes cannot be simple overall. (In theory it could be simple in everything that does not appertain to such processes, but, as these processes are increasingly brought to bear on nature itself, it becomes clear that the region of that which does not somehow appertain to them is continually diminished.) And so if it turns out that we require a highly complex theory to account for the ways of human thought, then nature itself cannot be all that simple. In the end it is nature's cognitive systematicity that provides an evidential indication—perhaps the best we can ever actually obtain: the systemic harmony of the real.

We explain the processes of nature in terms of efficient causes and the proceedings of people in terms of final users. And we explain the coordination between the two, not in terms of some preestablished harmony but through the fact that people are a part of nature and that the resort to aim and purposes—to final cases—is an efficient and effective mechanism of comportment from beings that evolution has inserted into nature in one sort of way, as intelligent beings into and on the basis of the information available to them. The systemic unity of science and culture roots just exactly where Henri Bergson thought it did—in the "creative" processes of evolution.

Inductive Principles as Instruments of Cognitive Harmonization

Induction as Cognitive Systematization

Dictionaries sometimes define the inductive reasoning on which factual inquiry relies in such terms as "inference from particular cases to a general conclusion." But such inferences—for example, from spaniels eat meat, schnauzers eat meat, and corgis eat meat, to all dogs eat meat—illustrate only one particularly straightforward sort of inductive reasoning. Nor will it do to add merely those further inferences to a particular conclusion that move from effects to causes: from the smoke to the fire, say, or from the bark to the dog. For even this does not go nearly far enough. Inferences from sample to population, from part to whole, from the jaw to the entire alligator, from style to authorship, from clue to culprit, from symptom to disease, are all also modes of inductive reasoning. The characteristic and crucial thing about inductive reasoning is that it is *ampliative* through overreaching the evidence in hand to move to conclusions lying beyond the informative range of relatively insufficient data. Inductive reasoning, in sum, seeks to provide plausible answers to questions where the deductive reach of the available information is insufficient.

Induction as we standardly practice it in everyday life and scientific inquiry is a matter of question resolution through the optimal systematization of experience—of answering our questions in terms of the most straightforward overall account that we are able to devise to accommodate the facts or presumptive facts that our observation of the world's phenomena (natural or artificially contrived in experimentation) places at our disposal. Induction is thus a fundamentally regulative and procedural resource for inquiry—one that proceeds by way of implementing the injunction: Maximize the extent to which your cognitive commitments are harmoniously systematic overall. In the absence of such a principle, or some functional equivalent of it, the venture of rational inquiry via empirical data will not get under way at all.

Induction is accordingly not so much a process of inference as one of estimation; its conclusions are not so much extracted from data as suggested by them. We clearly want to accomplish our explanatory gap filling in the least risky, the minimally problematic way, as determined by plausibilistic best-fit considerations. Induction jumps to its conclusion instead of literally deriving it from the given premises by drawing the conclusion from them through some extractive process. Long ago, William Whewell put this key point nicely: "Deduction," he wrote, "descends steadily and methodically, step by step. Induction mounts by a leap which is out of the reach of method (or, at any rate, mechanical routine). She bounds to the top of the stairs at once."[1] Of course, any such ampliative leaps beyond the evidence at hand entail further risks. (In this regard, a scientific revolution is like a market crash, when everything comes tumbling down in one great collapse.) Any inductive process is inherently chancy. Induction is always a matter of guesswork, and its results are always at risk to further or better data. But, of course, what is involved is responsible, rather than wild, guesswork—rational conjecture rather than fanciful speculations. To be sure, we cannot pass by any sort of strict inference or cognitive calculation from the premises of an inductive argument to its conclusion because (*ex hypothesi*) this would be a deductive non sequitur. An inductive conclusion (in the very nature of the case) asserts something well above and beyond the information contained in its premises.[2] Clearly, the standard and paradigmatic mode of inference—of deriving a conclusion from the information provided by premises—is actual deduction,[3] and this paradigm does not fit induction smoothly. As one philosopher has felicitously put it, our inductive "conclusions" are "not derived from the observed facts, but invented in order to account for them."[4]

Induction and the Economic Rationale of Simplicity Preference

Induction is a matter of projecting our cognitive commitments just as far beyond the data as is necessary to get answers to our questions. It seeks to stay as close to the data as possible while proceeding under the aegis of established principles of inductive systematization: simplicity, harmony, uniformity, and the rest. The ideas of economy and simplicity are the guiding principles of inductive reasoning, whose procedure is that of the precept, Resolve your cognitive problems in the simplest, most economical way compatible with an adequate use of the information at your disposal. Induction proceeds by way of constructing the most economical structures to house the available data comfortably. It seeks to discern the simplest overall pattern of regularity that can adequately accommodate our information regarding cases in hand and then projects it across the entire spectrum of possibilities in order to answer our general questions. Induction is a process of implementing the general idea of cognitive systematicity, building up the simplest information structure capable of resolving our cognitive problems in the light of what we take ourselves to know.

As a fundamentally inductive endeavor, scientific theorizing accordingly involves the search for, or the construction of, the least complex and most straightforward theory structure capable of adequately accommodating the currently available data. The key principle is that of economy of means for the realization of given cognitive ends, and the ruling injunction is that of cognitive economy—of getting the most informative answer we can obtain with the least effect of complication. Complexities cannot be ruled out, but they must always pay their way in terms of increased systemic adequacy!

In induction we exploit the information at hand to answer the

questions in the most straightforward (economical) way. Suppose, for
example, that we are asked to supply the next member of the series 1,
2, 3, 4, ... We shall straightaway respond with 5, supposing the series
to be simply that of the integers. Of course, the actual series might well
be 1, 2, 3, 4, 11, 12, 13, 14, 101, 102, 103, 104, ... And then the correct answer will eventuate as 11 rather than 5. Though we cannot rule
such possibilities out, they do not deter our inductive proceedings.
The inductively appropriate course lies with the production rule that
is the simplest answer: Add 1 to the number you have just produced.
In induction, we proceed to answer questions by opting for the simplest resolution that meets the conditions of the problem. And we do
this not because we know a priori that this simplest resolution will
prove to be correct. (We know no such thing!) We adopt this answer,
provisionally at least, just exactly because this is the simplest, the most
economical way of providing a resolution that does justice to the facts
and to the demands of the situation. We recognize that other possibilities exist but ignore them pro tem, exactly because there is no cogent
reason for giving them favorable notice at this stage.

It has long been recognized that simplicity is one aspect of systematicity that will play an especially prominent part in the methodology
of science, constituting a crucial cognitive value and a paramount factor in inductive reasoning. There is as widespread agreement as there
ever is in such foundational matters on the principle that simple
hypotheses enjoy a preferred status. But when one presses the question of validating this simplicity preference, one meets with discord
and disagreement. The matter becomes far less problematic, however,
once one approaches it from a methodological rather than a substantive point of view. Henri Poincaré has observed that "[even] those
who do not believe that natural laws must be simple are still often ob-
ligated to act as if they did believe it. They cannot entirely dispense
with this necessity without making all generalization, and therefore
all science, impossible. It is clear that any fact can be generalized in an
infinite number of ways, and it is a question of choice. The choice
can only be guided by considerations of simplicity. . . . To sum up,
in most cases every law is held to be simple until the contrary is
proved."[5] These observations are wholly right-minded. As cognitive

possibilities proliferate in the course of theory-building inquiry, a principle of choice and selection among alternatives becomes requisite. And here economy and its other systematic congeners—simplicity, uniformity, and the rest—are the natural guidelines. To be sure, whether the direction in which they point us is actually correct is something that remains to be seen. But they clearly afford the most natural and promising starting point. The simplest viable resolution of our problems is patently that which must be allowed to prevail, at any rate pro tem, until such time as its untenability becomes manifest and complications force themselves upon us. Where a simple solution will accommodate the data at hand, there is no good reason for turning elsewhere. It is a fundamental principle of rational procedure, operative just as much in the cognitive domain as anywhere else, that from among various alternatives that are anything like equally well qualified in other regards, we should adopt the one that is the simplest, the most economical—in whatever modes of simplicity and economy are relevant.

In inductive situations we are called on to answer questions whose resolution lies beyond the reach of information at hand. We simply have to transcend the data. And we do this by projecting our problem resolutions along the lines of least resistance. We try to economize our cognitive effort. We use the simplest workable means to our ends exactly because the others are harder to use. Whenever possible, we analogize the present case to other similar ones, because the introduction of new patterns complicates our cognitive repertoire. We use the simplest viable formulations because they are easier to remember and simpler to use. Insofar as possible, we try to ease the burdens we pose for our memory (for information storage and retrieval) and for our intellect (for information processing and calculation). We favor uniformity, analogy, simplicity, and the like because that lightens the burden of cognitive labor. When other things are anything like equal, simpler theories are bound to be economically more advantageous. We avoid needless complications whenever possible, because this is the course of an economy of effort. And just herein lies the justification of induction. For by its very nature induction affords us the most cost-effective—the economically optimal—means for accomplishing an essential cognitive task. With cognitive as with physical tools, complexities, disuniformities, abnormalities, and so on, are complications that exact a price, departures from the easiest resolution that must be motivated by some appropriate benefit, some situational pressure. Accordingly, the rationale of our inductive praxis is a fundamentally economic one.

Galileo wrote: "When therefore I observe a stone initially at rest falling from a considerable height and gradually acquiring new increases of speed, why should I not believe that such increments come about in the simplest, the most plausible way?"[6] Why not indeed? Subsequent findings may, of course, render this simplest position untenable. But this recognition only reinforces the stance that simplicity is not an inevitable hallmark of truth (*simplex sigillum veri*) but merely a methodological tool of inquiry—a guidepost of procedure. When something simple accomplishes the cognitive tasks in hand as well as some more complex alternative does, it is foolish to adopt the latter. After all, we need not presuppose that the world somehow is systematic (simple, uniform, and the like) to validate our penchant for the systematicity of our cognitive commitments. Our striving for cognitive systematicity in its various forms persists even in the face of complex phenomena: the commitment to simplicity in our account of the world remains a methodological desideratum regardless of how complex or untidy the world may turn out to be.

It is the universal practice in scientific theory construction, when other things are anything like equal, to give preference to
- one-dimensional rather than multidimensional modes of description,
- quantitative rather than qualitative characterizations,
- lower-order rather than higher-order polynomials,
- linear rather than nonlinear differential equations.

In each case, the former is somehow simpler than the latter alternative. To be sure, efforts to the contrary notwithstanding, no theoretician and no philosopher has managed to provide an adequate substantive characterization of simplicity, answering to the formula X is simpler than Y if they stand to one another in a relationship of just such-and-such a descriptive sort. But a methodological, or procedural, characterization is something far easier to come by. The comparatively simpler is simply that which is easier to work with, which overall is the more economical to operate when it comes to application and interaction. Simplicity on such a perspective is a concept of the practical order, pivoting simply on being more economical to use, that is, less demanding of resources.

The ideas of economy and simplicity are the guiding principles of inductive reasoning. The procedure is that of the precept: "Resolve your cognitive problems in the simplest, most harmonious way compatible with an adequate use of the information at your disposal." Our penchant for simplicity is easy to justify on grounds of economy. If one claims a phenomenon to depend not just on certain distances and weights and sizes, but also, say, on such further factors as temperature and magnetic forces, then one must design a more complex data-gathering apparatus to take readings over this enlarged range of physical parameters. Or, again, in a curve-fitting situation, compare the thesis that the appropriate function is linear with the thesis that it is linear up to a point and sinusoidally wavelike thereafter. Writing a set of instructions for checking whether empirically determined point coordinates fit the specified function is clearly a vastly less complex—and so more economical—process in the linear case.

The impetus of simplicity has one other important ramification. In life we must not only solve problems but also learn. Yet we must learn to walk before we can run, and learn to solve simple problems before we can solve complicated ones. In simplifying and indeed oversimplifying our problems, we adopt a good strategy for learning. Induction is on the side of cost-effectiveness economics in our cognitive operations.

Induction should accordingly be viewed as a cognitive process, or family of methods, for arriving at our best estimate of the correct answers to pressing questions, whose resolution transcends the reach of the facts in hand. Given the information transcendence at issue in such truth estimation, we cannot avoid realizing that an inductive procedure does not guarantee the truth of its products. Indeed, if the history of science has taught us any one thing, it is that the best estimate of the truth that we can make at any particular stage of the cognitive game is in general subsequently seen, with the wisdom of hindsight, as being far off the mark. Induction opts for simplicity, and its characteristic flaw is thus oversimplification. Nevertheless, the fact remains that the inductively indicated answer as elicited in light of the standard parameters of cognitive harmonization does afford our best available estimate of the true answer, in the sense that its adoption represents the best available way of resolving our cognitive problems with the materials at hand.

The Methodological Aspect of Inductive Economy

On such a view, the systemic harmony of inductive reasoning is best approached with reference, not to reality as such, or even to our conception of it, but more accurately to the ways and means we employ in conceptualizing it. Simplicity preference, for example, is based on the strictly method-oriented practical consideration that the simple hypotheses are the most convenient and advantageous for us to put to use in the context of our purposes. There is thus no recourse to a substantive (or descriptively constitutive) postulate of the simplicity of nature; it suffices to have recourse to a regulative (or practical) precept of economy of means. And the pursuit of cognitive systematicity is ontologically neutral. It is noncommittal on matters of substance; it merely reflects the procedure of conducting our question-resolving endeavors with the greatest economy. In inquiry as elsewhere, a principle of least effort predominates; rationality enjoins us to employ the maximally economic means to the attainment of chosen ends. Such an approach constitutes a theoretical defense of inductive systematically, which in fact rests on practical considerations.

Simpler (more systematic) answers are more easily codified, taught, learned, used, investigated, and so on. In short, they are more economical to operate. In consequence, the regulative principles of convenience and economy in learning and inquiry suffice to provide a rational basis for systematicity preference. Our penchant for simplicity, uniformity, and systematicity in general is not a matter of a substantive theory regarding the nature of the world but one of search strategy—of cognitive methodology. In sum, we opt for simplicity (and systematicity in general) in inquiry because it is teleologically effective for the more cost-efficient realization of the goals of the enterprise, for the parameters of inductive systematicity—simplicity, uniformity, regularity, normality, coherence, and the rest—all represent practical principles of cognitive economy.[7] They are labor-saving devices for the avoidance of complications in the course of our endeavors to realize the objects of inquiry. The rationale of simplicity preference is straightforward. It lies in the single word *economy*. The simplest workable solution is that which is the easiest, most straightforward, most inexpensive one to work with. It is the very quintessence of foolishness to expend greater resources than are necessary for the achievement of our governing objectives. And by its very nature, induction affords us the most cost-effective—the economically optimal—means for accomplishing an essential cognitive task. The rational basis for our inductive simplicity preference accordingly lies in considerations of the economic dimension of practice and procedure, rather than in any factual supposition about the world's nature.

It is indeed economy and convenience that determine our regulative predilection for simplicity and systematicity in general. Our prime motivation is to get by with a minimum of complication, to adopt strategies of question resolution that enable us, among other things (1) to continue with existing solutions unless and until the epistemic circumstances compel us to introduce changes (uniformity), (2) to make the same processes do as great a variety of scientific tasks as possible (generality), and (3) to keep to the simplest process that will do the job (simplicity). Such a perspective combines the commonsensical precept, Try the simplest thing first, with this principle of burden of proof: Maintain your cognitive commitments until there is good reason to abandon them.[8] It clearly makes eminent sense to move onward from the simplest (least complex) available solution to introduce further complexities when and as—but only when and as—they are forced upon us.

The penchant for inductive systematicity reflected in the structural dimension of information is accordingly a matter of striving for economy in the conduct of inquiry. It is governed by an analogue of Occam's Razor—a principle of parsimony to the effect that needless complexity is to be avoided. Given that the inductive method, viewed in its practical and methodological aspect, aims at the most efficient and effective means of question resolution, it is only natural that our inductive precepts should direct us toward the most systematic, and thereby economical, device that can actually do the job at hand. Our systematizing procedures pivot on this injunction always to adopt the most economical (simple, general, straightforward) solution that meets the demands of the situation. The root principle of inductive systematization is the axiom of cognitive economy: *complicationes non multiplicandae sunt praeter necessitatem.* The other-things-equal preferability of simpler solutions over more complex ones is thus obvious enough: they are less cumbersome to store, easier to take hold of, and less difficult to work with.

From this perspective, then, simplicity preference emerges as a matter of simplification of labor, a matter of the intellectual economy of cognitive procedure. Why use a more complex solution where a simple one will do as well? Why depart from uniformity? Why use a new, different solution where an existing one will serve? The good workman selects his tools with a view to (1) their versatility (power, efficacy, adaptability, and the like), and (2) their convenience (ease of use), and other similar factors of functional adequacy to the task in hand. Simplicity preference, accordingly, emerges as a means of implementing the precepts of economy of operation in the intellectual sphere. Its initial advantages are not substantive/ontological but methodological/pragmatic in orientation. The crucial fact is that simplicity preference is a cognitive policy recommended by considerations of cost effectiveness; in the setting of the cognitive purposes at issue, it affords a maximally advantageous inquiry mechanism.

Rules Versus Principles

In the normal course of things rules of procedure are conditional injunctions that indicate specific steps to be taken in various circumstances. They generally take the form, "In circumstances of such-and-such a sort, do (or do not do) this or that." A principle, by contrast, does not tell one what specifically is to be done, but only gives generalized guidance. "Do not lie" is a rule ("When conveying information to someone, tell them the truth"). "Honor your father and mother" is a principle—its implementation requires a further and complex set of directions as to what "honoring" people involves and what is appropriate in this regard with respect to parents.

Principles do not prescribe particular actions or courses of action; they stipulate directions. They do not specify concrete steps but generalized objectives, indicating the necessity or desirability of a certain generalized tendency.

The function of principles is thus to guide the process of decision making. Unlike rules, they do not purport to make our decisions for us but only canalize them in certain general directions. Thus, take the following principle of rationality: "Treat like cases alike." Suppose we have two cases of thought or action, A and B. Are they alike in the issue-relevant respects? That all depends—the principles certainly will not tell us. And even if they are, what are we to do in case A? Again, the principle does not tell us what to do; all it says is that whatever it is appropriate to do in case A will then also be appropriate in a similar case B. The principle does not dictate a course of action: it serves to delimit the range of appropriateness.

As a typical example in this regard, consider the logical principle of contradiction: "Avoid contradictions; keep your commitments consistent; never assert both p and not-p." Or, again, it is, no doubt, a worthy and appropriate principle not to put the lives of people needlessly at risk. But the issue of what should concretely be done to realize this generalized desideratum is left subject to complex and circumstantially variable conditions.

Principles are accordingly thus more abstract and general than rules. The injunctions they involve proceed along such lines as:

> In the normal and ordinary course of things, barring nonstandard and extraordinary conditions, endeavor to facilitate the realization of such-and-such a condition of things.

Every practice has its principles. For everything that can be done can be done better and worse in more or less effective ways. And principles provide our guidance here. Accordingly, principles are guidelines for doing well rather than specifically for doing good. For even modes of practice that are inherently negative—burglary, for example, or forgery—will be subject to principles. The value standing of principles depends on that of the practice at issue. Whenever the competent/incompetent distinction can take hold, there will be room for principles.

Why Principles?

Why should there be principles? Why not get by with rules alone? Because in a complex world the range of cases and circumstances is so vast and variegated that no set of explicit rules could adequately cover the range of possibilities. There are exceptions to all or at any rate most rules, and without the guidance of principles we would not be able to proceed appropriately on the basis of rules alone.

But why not do without principles and just make ad hoc decisions on the basis of the specifics of the case?

1. Cases share commonalties and there is no point in reinventing the wheel (economy of operation).
2. Rationality (let alone fairness) calls for treating like cases alike (rational and ethical uniformity).
3. Cases are complex and we need guidance in handling them; presumption facilitates process (rational economy).

Principles do and must exist in the space of rational operation intermediate between the unavailingness of available rules and the vacuity of rule-devoid guidance.

Taxonomy: Classifying Principles

Principles govern the doings of agents. And in general such doings fall into three main categories: thought, action, and evaluation. Correspondingly we will have cognitive principles, practical principles, and normative principles.

Sometimes, to be sure, there are transcategorematic principles that reach across such classificatory divides. Take the principle, "Proceed with greater care and caution in matters when the stakes at issue are greater." Not only does this principle hold good in all three domains of thought, action, and evaluation, but it fuses two of them tighter, namely, action ("proceed") and evaluation ("greater of lesser stakes").

Every modus operandi—every practice of process of doing something of whatever sort—will be subject to principles. The taxonomy of principles will accordingly be endlessly complex. There are principles of arithmetic, of chess, of gardening, and so on. To deal with principles in detail one will, accordingly, have to limit one's horizons to one or another of these definitive and delimited domains.

It is thus easy to find illustrations of cogent principles of various kinds; for example:

Cognitive principles: "Align your belief with the best available evidence"; "keep your beliefs compatible with one another."

Ethical principles: "Treat others as you would have them treat you"; "never decide your actions with reference to your interests alone ('what is in it for me?'), without heed of their potential impact on the interests of others."

Communicative principles: "Do not waste your interlocutors time"; "do not put forth misleading or deceptive messages."

Principles of common courtesy: "Do not needlessly offend the sensibilities of your interagents"; "in any multilateral effort, do your fair share."

Hierarchy

There will certainly be principles of a higher order that can trump the applicability of others. The leading principle of the Hippocratic Code wears its paramountcy on its sleeves: "First, do no harm." The "Prime Directive" for the space explorers of the fictional *Starship Enterprise* was "Do not interfere with an alien civilization's development." Most moralists (though doubtless not all) would agree that "Do not endanger the lives of people" trumps "Do not tell falsehoods." Principles are not created equal. Some relate to situations where greater issues are at stake than is the case with others and accordingly have greater weight.

Whence Principles?

The operative principles will invariably be subject to the teleology of the particular practice involved, be it intelligible communication, philosophical deliberation, or read construction. In every case the mission and reason for being of principles will root in their capacity to possibilize and/or facilitate realization of the objectives of the enterprise. Principles are thus instrumentalities and as such their rationale is always pragmatic (in the broader sense of this term).

Principles Issue from Two Styles of Reflection: Top Down and Bottom Up

The top-down discernment of principles is a matter of reflecting on the general aims and principles of the enterprise at issue and noting—be it through analysis or intuition—that these require conducting the business of the domain in a certain sort of way with certain ends and objectives kept in view. This is ultimately a matter of *functional analysis* because teleological considerations will be paramount here.

By contrast the bottom-up discernment of principles proceeds by looking at the manifold of available rules and scrutinizing them for commonalties, consonances, and convergences. The justificatory process here is based on the second for a general thread of tendency and direction that is universal or at least widely common among the rules.

The various approaches accordingly engender three rather different modes of justificatory procedure: top down, bottom up, and dialectical.

The Top-Down Model

Principles come first in the order of logical priority. They get established on the basis of abstract and general considerations. Specific rules are thus articulated to implement the principles. And concrete decisions and actions are then generally aimed at by following the rules.

The Bottom Up Model

Concrete cases have priority; it is they that come first. We make decisions in concrete matters on the basis of their case-specific features. Rules and principles emerge by inductive generalizations from concrete cases: they simply reflect discernible patterns among concrete cases in a particular realm of practice.

The Dialectical Model

The relationship between particular decisions and actions, on the one hand, and the rules and principles that govern them, on the other, is not one of priority at all but of interdependence. There is no order of fundamentality here. Any realm of rational practice involves both. It does not matter where we begin; sooner or later we arrive both at concrete actions and decisions and a group of the manifold of rules and principles that guide them.

The Issue of Consistency

These three approaches to principle justification bear very differently on the issue of the consistency and compatibility of principles. The top-down process of principle validation with its essentially subsumptive approach to principles sees it as essential for coherent thought that principles be consistent. The inconsistency of general principles is unacceptable, as it itself is a matter of general principle.

The bottom-up process of principle-validation consistency is once again demanded—but now as a matter of methodological and procedural strategy. That is, we carry on the process of abstraction and generalization in such a way that consistency is ensured.

Finally, the dialectical approach, with its emphasis on reciprocal interdependence, works itself out differently. It looks to a more complex interrelationship where different and potentially conflicting principles may best and most smoothly accord with different sorts of cases and situations. Accordingly, it contemplates the prospect that a variegated body of practice may well involve a variety of principles that stand in a relationship of reciprocal tension and conflict. On this basis, however, the principles that canalize a practice need not be consistent. Take *proverbial wisdom* as an illustrative example. Proverbs are intended to provide us with guidance for life. But life is complex. No simple rules are satisfactory; an approach or procedure that works in some cases will fail miserably in others. So proverbial wisdom has to be attuned to move in either direction in line with the almost infinitely complex and ramified character of different circumstances and situations. If there is to be any body of simple rules at all, it must, if adequate, be prepared to move in opposite directions subject to the indications of diversified circumstances.

The most striking and significant feature of proverbial wisdom is its inconsistency. It is Janus-faced in its tendency to look in opposite directions at once, reminiscent of Newton's first law, in that for every proverb of one tendency there is another with equal force of the opposite tendency, as attested by the following pairs: A stitch in time saves nine / Look before you leap; Beware of Greeks bearing gifts / Don't look a gift horse in the mouth; Look after the pennies, and the pounds will look after themselves / You can't take it with you; *Plus ça change, plus c'est la même chose / Tempora mutantur, nos et mutatur in illis.* Proverbs that point in opposite directions mark the complexity of human life: that there is time to hurry ("A stitch in time saves nine") and a time for being slow ("Haste makes waste"); that "depending on conditions," both ways of proceeding are proper and well advised. In all such contexts where principles can come into conflict we require or at least desire metaprinciples, that is to say, principles for deciding which principles have priority in situations of the type at issue.

In the absence of the guidance of such principles we have little alternative but to have recourse to informal judgment to effect a resolution as to comparative primacy and priority. Some specific examples of sensible metaprinciples are:

- Do not ignore relevant principles.
- Apply only relevant principles.
- Always refer your rules of action to the appropriate principles.

- Never act in defiance of the pertinent principles.
- Conflicts among principles are settled not by compromise (partition) but by prioritization (dominance).
- Economy: do not bring in more than you need.

Is there a hierarchical regress, with principles governing principles for principle usage? No, because there is no need for them.

Optional versus Mandatory Practices

Our concept of ethical comportment is such as to require people to keep their actions in consonance with the principles that are inherently fitting and appropriate. Characterizing someone as "a man of principle" is thus seen as an approbation, and characterizing him as "unprincipled," a derogation.

The here-operative distinction between optimal and mandatory practices is reflected in the difference between categorical and conditional principles. A principle of chess such as "Protect your king" is a conditional one: it holds for those who play chess when engaged in doing so, which they may or may not choose to do in a particular place and time. By contrast the principles of maintaining health or acting morally or thinking rationally are categorical. Since the processes and justice at issue (living, interacting, thinking) are not optimal for us but inherently programmed into the human situation, the principles involved are categorically mandatory for us. The principles of competent skating or lawyering or gardening apply only to those who choose to engage in the endeavor. But the categorical principles at issue with the activities that we inevitably offer members of our species are unconditionally categorical.

Accordingly, what makes moral principles binding is that ethically appropriate behavior is mandatory for rational agents at large. Most sorts of principles are only conditionally and contingently applicable. The principles of chess only apply for chess players, the principles of seamanship only for seamen. By contrast the principles of ethics or of logic do not admit of suspension. Thinking and acting are practices we cannot opt out of.

How Are Principles Justified?

Principles stipulate a certain consonance and uniformity of procedure. In this generic way all principles are principles of harmonization enjoining that what is done here be done there in similar circumstances as well. The characteristic work of principles is thus to coordinate—to harmonize.

How are principles justified? How do we determine their appropriateness? Basically, in two ways: reasoning and experience. Since principles function in the guidance of practice, they are teleological in their bearing. Practices and procedures are always purposively end-oriented: They are designed with a view of realizing some objective or other. And herein lies the key to the validation of principles.

Purposive/pragmatic justification has three characteristic modes:

1. A theoretical (general principally) necessary condition (*conditio sue qua non*); unfeasibility/impossibility of realizing the objective without knowing the mandate of the principle: "this or nothing."

2. Theoretical optimality; "this or nothing better"; no more promising alternative in view for guidance to goal-realization.

3. Proven efficiency; comparative optimality through trial and error.

What is operative throughout is a matter of pragmatics, of functional or purpose-oriented validation. The validation of principles proceeds through their giving useful guidance by promoting efficacy and efficiency in goal realization. Appropriate principles achieve this status in the first instance through their role in fostering the picture at issue, and in the second, higher instance through considering the capacity of that practice itself to foster the realization of the human good.

Knowledge pivots on generalization. We describe through shareable properties, we classify through kinds, we explain through laws. But all of these different modes of coordination operate through principles. For principles are, among other things, higher-level procedural generalizations: rules for rules. And in cognition, as elsewhere, our employment of the various modes of coordinative processes are themselves coordinated through principles. Consider, for example, the so-called principle of contradiction with its pivotal injunction to avoid inconsistencies, to avert doing in one place or on one occasion that which contradicts or conflicts with that done elsewhere. Be it in matters of assertion and denial, in matters of action or in matters of evaluation the demands of this principle are operative throughout.

Rational Economy as the Gateway to Cognitive Principles

And so cognitive principles one and all are ultimately rooted in the same functionally oriented rationale. For the domain over which they are operative has a purposive chamber, and the validation of principles consists uniformly in the consideration that this domain's definitive purpose or function is realized more effectively and efficiently than otherwise under the guidance of the principle at hand.

In other words, principles are in the end instrumentalities in the service of rational economy. Their validation pivots throughout on the idea that the relevant range of purpose is best served by proceeding in line with the relevant principles. To proceed in a domain of thought or action without due heed to the principles that are appropriate there is to ask for trouble, to make life harder for oneself than it needs to be. And this, of course, constitutes a profound failure in cultivating the harmony that rational economy demands.

The centrality of rational economy in the validation of principles creates a special place for the conception of simplicity in its justificatory role in matters of inductive reasoning. This large and important issue deserves a chapter unto itself.

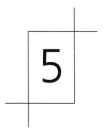

5

Harmony and a Sense of Proportion
in Cognitive Evaluation

Proportionalism

Harmony requires the mutual accommodation of constituents. For this reason proportion is a key element of harmony, and proportionalism is a fundamental and pervasive factor in human affairs. In matters of justice it calls for aligning the punishment with the gravity of the offense and aligning rewards with the magnitude of the contribution. In matters of inquiry it calls for aligning belief with the weight of evidence. And in managing our scientific inquiries it calls for aligning the allocation of resources with the importance of the issues at hand—for dedicating to the issues the share of care, concern, and attention that is their due by virtue of their importance in the larger scheme of things. In these regards and many more, proportionalism is a fundamental principle of rational procedure and a pivotal factor in cognitive harmonization at large. However, this chapter will focus specifically on the question of how this basic principle functions with respect to scientific knowledge.

Scientific Importance

Scientific progress is clearly determined not merely through the numerical proliferation of findings but through their size—not through their mere numbers but through the magnitude of their importance in the larger scheme of things. It is clear that without the distinction between the important and the unimportant at our disposal, we would be unable to adequately understand, successfully teach, or effectively practice science.

Of course, the distinction between theoretical/cognitive and practical/applicative importance must be drawn from the outset. Importance for explanatory purposes—for understanding—is something different from importance for practical purposes, that is, for useful applications. It is the former alone that will be at issue here. We are here concerned with the issue of importance *for understanding the ways of the world,* rather than a more specifically purpose-contextualized objective, such as "importance for increasing agricultural output" or "importance for diagnosing cancer." There is no doubt that such practical importance represents a significant issue. But it differs from theoretical importance and as such must be considered elsewhere.

Perhaps the most critical fact about scientific importance is that it represents an index of quality: of comparative significance in the context of understanding. Importance is thus a *comparative* conception: one thing is more important than another in that it claims and deserves a larger amount of attention and respect. Importance is therefore an inherently elitist conception: there is nothing democratic about it.

One recent philosopher of science who has touched on our subject is Karl Popper, who writes: "We want more than mere truth [in science]: what we look for is interesting truth—truth which is hard to come by. But in the natural sciences . . . what we look for is truth which has a high degree of explanatory power, which implies that it is logically improbable."[1] The difficulty here is that logical improbability must inevitably be assessed against a body of background premises, which, in the present case, can only mean the antecedent knowledge of belief. This circumstance coordinates importance with surprise value. Now, while this is plausible as far as it goes (we would clearly be disinclined to deem a totally unsurprising finding as important), it shipwrecks on the consideration that we can also be surprised in the context of entirely unimportant issues. If all our prior considerations point to X and nevertheless not-X turns out to be so, this can happen in small and trivial contexts as well as with big and significant ones. Among the few contemporary philosophers of science who have also written about scientific importance is Larry Laudan, who, in *Progress and Its Problems,* rightly observes that "the literature of the methodology of science offers us neither a taxonomy of its types of scientific problems, nor any acceptable method of grounding their relative importance."[2] However, Laudan himself is better at diagnosis than therapy: his discussion offers us various examples of important problems, but no effective criteria for what it is that constitutes this virtue. For, in essence, Laudan sees problems as important to the extent that currently fashionable theories disagree about them, but unfortunately this idea shipwrecks in the circumstance that theories can disagree about smaller issues as well as large ones. To understand scientific importance one will have to look in other directions.

Perhaps the most basic consideration on the subject is that being cognitively important is something rather different from being interesting. For interestingness is subjective, that is, it depends on what an individual is interested in, relates to what someone happens to find interesting. Scientific importance, by contrast, is an impersonal issue. It pivots on the matter of securing a clear and cogent account of nature's modus operandi. And this in turn reflects how prominent a role a fact or finding deserves and would accordingly demand in an adequate exposition of an area of inquiry.[3] Importance, therefore, does—or should—represent an objective issue.

So understood, the crux of importance is the matter of understanding—of the negotiation between fact and mind. Cognitive importance is a concept that belongs not to abstract logic but to the domain of information management. The importance of a fact hinges on the answer to the question, How large an overall loss by way of unknowing or confusion would be created for our grasp of a certain domain if this fact were lost from sight? The crucial point here is that scientific importance consists in making a difference for adequate understanding. It is a matter of the gap that would be left in the body of our presumed knowledge if the item at issue were lost. How is this idea to be made more precise?

The Quantification of Scientific Importance

How are we to proceed in practice in assessing the importance of scientific findings—and, above all, how might we be able to measure this? To maintain that one fact or finding is more important than another within the problem-setting of a particular subject-matter domain is to make a judgment of worth or value: it is to say that one finding merits a greater expenditure of intellectual resources—of attention, concern, time, and effort to discover, learn, explain, and teach—than another. Importance is accordingly a fundamentally economic concept—one of the pivotal concepts of the rational economy of cognition. The crux here is an essentially seismological standard based on the question, If the concept or thesis at issue were abrogated or abandoned, how large would be the ramifications and implications of this circumstance? How extensive would be the shocks and tremors reverberating throughout the whole range of what we (presumably) know?[4] Along such a line of thought, the "importance" of a factual issue will turn in the final analysis on how substantial an alteration in our body of scientific beliefs is wrought by our grappling with it, that is, the extent to which resolving the question at issue causes geological tremors reverberating across the cognitive landscape.

Importance accordingly is *a comparative concept of intellectual economy:* it represents the extent to which one thing deserves more attention (time, effort, energy) than another. The crucial thing for importance is thus inherent in the question of *how much*—how prominent a place in the sun does a certain idea or concept deserve. This is best viewed *in the light of the idea of a perfected textbook for the domain at issue*—a textbook that provides an ideally clear, cogent, and accurate systematization of the principles, theses, and theories of the field of inquiry at issue, elucidating for the benefit of serious students the considerations required for an accurate understanding of the composition and modus operandi of the domain. And it is space allocation in such an idealized systematization that best affords an index of importance. And in this regard it merits reemphasis to note that the crucial determinative factor for increasing importance is the extent of seismic disturbance of the cognitive terrain. In revising our textbook into a reconstituted harmonious whole, would we have to add or re-write a whole chapter, a section, a paragraph, a sentence, or a mere foot-note?

To be sure, space allocation will be demanded by some factors that, on the surface, seem to have little relevance to importance—complexity and difficulty, for example. But, of course, complications and difficulties are introduced in science only when and insofar as is required for obtaining an adequate and coherent overall account of the relevant facts. And such factors as difficulty and complexity will, accordingly, represent back doors to importance. In a good exposition of a domain, matters that are difficult to teach and to understand are always there for a reason—and these reasons will in general turn back to matters of importance.

Scientific importance is therefore not a qualitative but a relational feature, a function of how one item (fact, idea) relates to the others. It is a matter of proportion—of discursive prominence by way of space allocation in the context of systematization: When something is important, then a lot else depends on its being the way it is, and this is bound to be reflected in how much occasion there is to have recourse to it in the course of an adequate systematization of the domain at issue. This approach inflects a fundamentally pragmatic perspective. It views cognitive objects, such as concepts, ideas, and theories, as *tools*. And with any sort of production process—be it physical or cognitive—the importance of a tool lies in how much occasion there is to use it.

The systematic articulation of a cognitive domain is bound to reflect the structure of importance within its boundaries. In a strongly unified field, such as a mathematical axiom system, virtually everything depends on those axioms: they will be at work explicitly or obliquely at every stage of the discussion. But in a field whose information structure is compartmentalized and disaggregated, even the most significant items will have an importance that is no more than localized.

We thus arrive at what might be characterized as *the ideal space-allocation standard of importance*. A scientific idea, concept, principle, thesis, theory, finding, or fact is important exactly to the comparative extent that it merits space allocation in a perfected exposition of its field. Since importance in such a sense, as already noted, is a fundamentally economic conception, it encounters the economically pivotal factor of limits or finitude. But now the crucial factor is not, as is more usual, *absolute* size but *comparative* size. It is a matter of proportion—of deserving this-and-so much of the overall pie. And the cardinal principle in this regard is that no matter how large or small a pie is, there is only one of it to go around. All we can ever partition of anything is 100 percent of it. And so if one fact or finding deserves an additional 1 percent of the overall pie of attention and concern, then this has to be taken away from something else. To assign more importance to one thing is to attribute less importance to another. This being so, it follows that importance is a matter of percentage shares. In attributing importance we are playing a zero sum game.[5]

Importance in Quantitative Perspective

One key mechanism for implementing the idea of importance lies in the general principle that the comparative size of an elite (at any given level of eliteness) is determined by a fixed percentage. On this basis we straightaway obtain a definite and perspicuous relationship between the size of a population (P) and the size of an elite (E). And we will take an iterative approach here, via the line that an nth-order elite is the elite existing within an $(n-1)$st-order elite. As a result we have the situation shown in display 1. At issue here is a kind of cognitive Richter scale of importance based on the idea of successive orders of magnitude. Let us apply this idea to elite findings, that is, to important contributors:

DISPLAY 1
A hierarchy of elites

Level 1 $E_1 = kP$ (with $0 < k < 1$)
Level 2 $E_2 = k^2 P$
. . .
Level n $E_n = k^n P$

Quality Distribution

To elucidate the implications of this approach to the cognitive importance of a scientific issue or problem, let us consider the matter from the perspective of a more-or-less average scientific/technical book or monograph. Of such a treatise we can say that it is going to be divided into chapters, sections, paragraphs, and sentences. For the sake of discussion, we may suppose that display 2 roughly captures the situation.

DISPLAY 2
A hypothetical treatise

Ten chapters per book
Ten sections per chapter
Ten paragraphs per section
Ten sentences per paragraph
Ten words per sentence

The result will be a more-or-less standard book of some $10^5 = 100,000$ words or 250 pages. In terms of space allocation we will then have the situation shown in display 3.

DISPLAY 3
Space allocation in our hypothetical treatise

One book, 100%	level 1
One chapter, approx. 10%	level 2
One section, approx. 1%	level 3
One paragraph, approx. 0.1%	level 4
One sentence, approx. 0.01%	level 5

Note that, in general, we have it that one level n unit merits a space allocation of approximately $1000\%/10^n$.

If space allotment reflects importance (a big assumption, this, and one that is highly idealized), then our book will contain ideas or findings at the level of magnitude indicated in display 4. Cognitive importance is thus reflected in the allocation of resources (space, time, energy) in an idealized approach to information management.

DISPLAY 4
Quality levels

1. One big (first importance) idea for the book as a whole
2. Ten sizeable (second importance) ideas, one for each chapter
3. One hundred moderately (third importance) ideas, one for each section
4. One thousand smallish (fourth importance) ideas, one for each paragraph
5. Ten thousand elemental (fifth importance) ideas, one for each sentence

---

Building on this illustration, let us follow through somewhat further on the above-mentioned idea that we can measure the quality level of fact/findings through their "magnitude," as shown in display 5.

DISPLAY 5
Quantity and Quality

A fact/finding in a given field has the quality magnitude:	If it deserves this percentage of our total attention/concern—that is, time and space—within this field:
1	100% ($= 10^2$)

3	1% ($= 10^0$)
4	0.1% ($=10^{-1}$)
n	10^{3-n}%

In our example, then, if a field has N items, then the number of items of quality magnitude n for which it has room is

$$\text{Items}_N(n) = N\,5\,10^{1-n},$$

with each such nth magnitude finding occupying 10^{3-n} percent of the overall space allocated and thereby ideally engrossing a proportionate amount of the overall importance of what is at issue.

The quality structure of a domain could accordingly be mapped out in general by dividing it into successive groups of constituents at different quality levels, as in display 6.

DISPLAY 6
The quality structure of a domain

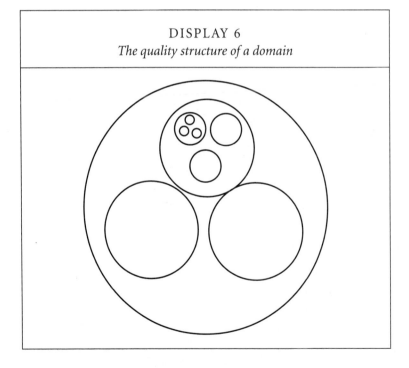

What we have here is a picture of nested aggregation with findings at a given level of quality in point of importance encompassing a multitude of others at lower levels of quality. With this picture in view, it is easy to see how findings at different levels of importance can encompass others by way of consequences, presuppositions, consistency, evidentiation, or the like. And, of course, our book analogy could be replicated on a larger scale in such a sequence as cognitive domain, discipline, substantive, specialty, problem area, problem, problem component. But, throughout, importance is directly reflected in terms of space allocation. The presently contemplated spatiometric-proportionality approach to importance is thus predicated on the idea that the importance of an item within a given domain of deliberations is simply an index of the comparative amount of attention it deserves and thereby of the comparative amount of space that would be devoted to it in a fully adequate exposition of the domain at issue.

Estimated versus Actual and Real versus Apparent

This understanding of domain-relative importance can be readily enlarged—at least in theory—by contemplating the idea of an idealized "perfected scientific library" in which the totality of domains of deliberation would be comprehensively encompassed. In this library each domain of factual knowledge would be given its canonically definitive systematization—its perfected account in terms of correctness and completeness.

This model of a perfected library is—to be sure—something very different from the Borges library contemplated by the Argentinean polymath Luis Borges. For the Borges library is universal: it deals not only with actuality but seeks to map out the realm of possibility as well; accordingly, the vast bulk of its holdings will be works of fiction rather than of science. Our perfected scientific library, by contrast, concerns itself with fact alone and leaves fiction aside.

Of course, the constitution of even our more modest library involves a vast amount of idealization. This simply reflects the fact that it is real rather than putative importance that has been the focus of our concern. If we want to come down from the fanciful level of idealization that this involves, then we must deal with the reality of actual science libraries in place of that idealization. We must, in short, take the Hegelian line that the real is rational, and that the reality of things stands surely for that otherwise unattainable idealization.

The *importance* of a question or answer that arises in one state-of-the-art state is something that can only be discovered with hindsight from the vantage point to which the attempts to grapple with it had led us. In science, apparently insignificant problems (the blue color of the sky, or the anomalous excess of background radiation) can acquire great importance once we have a state-of-the-art that makes them instances of important new effects that instantiate or indicate major theoretical innovations. It is only when a finding is stated, explained, and codified as thought absorption into the expository corpus of science that its importance will become evident.

This being so, it should be clear that when we ourselves actually engage in the business of attributing importance to facts and findings we are providing *estimates* of importance. Importance for science as we have it here and now is one sort of thing—namely, putative or estimated and thus subjective importance—whereas real, objective importance is a matter of how matters stand in ideal or perfected science, for the crucial fact is that progressiveness, insignificance, importance, interest, and the like are all concepts that must, in practice, be regarded as state-of-the-art relative conceptions. And in consequence, as far as we are concerned, an item's cognitive importance must be taken to hinge on the question of how critical it is in securing an adequate understanding of the subject-matter domain at issue *as this domain stands here and now*. And this means that we are constrained to proceeding at the level of estimation by dealing with apparent rather than actual importance.

For all practical purposes, then, it will not be "ideally deserved" space allocation that is our working index of importance but actual space allocations in the actually existing literature. In assessing importance, we have no choice but to work with actual libraries rather than the hypothetical perfected library. And our findings with respect to actual libraries will have to be acknowledged as representing no more than imperfect *estimates* for matters regarding the perfected library.

The Role of Citation

In thought as in travel we have to begin from where we are. Given the facts of life we have no alternative but to see science as we have it representing our best available estimate of ideal science. (A thesis would not belong to our campus of *putative* truth if we did not regard it as our best available estimate of the *real* truth.) Accordingly, the scientific literature *as it is* affords our best achievable view of the scientific literature as it ought to be. And this means that for adjusting importance we can do no better than to look to the literature of science and to let its structure be our guide.

On this basis, our most practicable and available approach to importance is through citation studies. For now the comparative amount of space allocation—which we can assess by the number and length of citations—will serve as our effective measure of importance.[6] But a substantial array of studies of citation statistics confirm the picture of display 7. The same drastic picture of exponential decline obtains on both sides, and so importance can just as effectively be estimated in terms of prominence in citation space as by prominence in discussion space.[7] Given that *science as we actually have it* represents our best available *estimate* of *science as it would ideally be developed,* the two can be viewed in practice as representing two sides of the same coin. For we have little sensible alternative to accepting the literature of science *as it stands* as our best available approximation to science *as it ought to be.*[8]

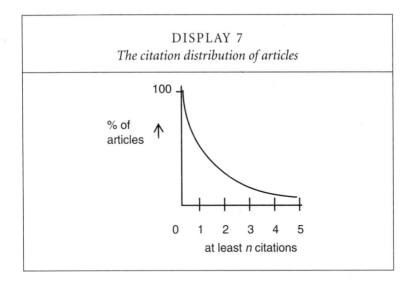

DISPLAY 7
The citation distribution of articles

Another perspective on the issue is also instructive in this regard. It relates to what has come to be called Price's law, which states that if a discipline is cultivated by K researchers, then half of the work in the field will be produced by a prolific elite of size $\sqrt{K}$. If this is even close to being the case, then a literature-proportionate conception of scientific importance is bound to see this elite as constituting the important workers in the discipline—that is, those who accomplish a disproportionately large share of the important work.

The established etiquette governing the modus operandi of scientific publication has two critically important features in this regard: it coordinates findings (ideas, principles, theories) with the names of their discoverers; and it mandates giving people credit for findings that are relevant by way of evidentiation, presumption, or consequence. The names mentioned thus reflect the cognitively relevant findings. And this means that short of using citation indexes one could also proceed by using the name indexes of texts and handbooks to estimate importance, with bibliographic aids also affording an oblique approach to estimating the importance of findings.

No one can doubt that the use of citation statistics is an imperfect method for estimating importance given that many sorts of issue-distorting influences can come into play—fads and fashions prominent among them. But as a useful resource for the first approximation in providing what is admittedly no more than an estimate, there seems to be no more plausible and more manifestly impersonal place to start.

Let us review the various alternatives here and compare the options. The literature reveals but three ways of evaluating the importance of scientific findings:
- importance as improbability (Popper);
- importance as innovativeness, as departure from currently accepted views (Laudan); and
- importance as comparative prominence in the idealized literature (Rescher).

The first runs into the problem that there is no realistic and reasonable way of assessing the inherent probability of theories. The second runs into the problem that while novelty may be an index of something's being interesting, its being important will have to depend on other factors, because innovation is possible in small as in large matters.[9] The third has the shortcoming that it deals with an idealization, but this can be offset by the consideration that here as elsewhere we can take the real to stand as surrogate for the idea.

Thus, all of the available alternatives have their shortcomings. But it should be clear that once the issue of assessing importance is seen in terms of *estimation* rather than of *determination,* this third approach offers the best prospects.

A Dialectical Digression

A brief digression into methodology becomes unavoidable at this point. In clarifying the concept of scientific importance, as with other terminology coherent concepts, one confronts three issues:
- What does it *mean* to call something an X?
- What sort of standard *authorizing evidence* entitles one to call something an X?

- What reason is there to think that the authorizing evidence at issue is adequate to the meaning at hand.

Accordingly, we need to inquire about (1) meaning or truth conditions, (2) evidentiation or use conditions, and (3) a rationale of adequation that coordinates the second condition to the first.

Where does the issue of scientific importance stand in this regard? On the side of meaning conditions we have seen that its crux is a matter of space allocation in *ideal* science. On the side of use conditions, by contrast, we have noted that since the realm of the ideal and perfected is inaccessible to us, use conditions pivot on the issue of space collection in actual (rather than ideal) science as best it can be assessed through citation indexes and other statistical bibliographic aids. This leaves the question of the conformity between the two. Why should it be that science-as-we-actually-have-it is our best available estimative surrogate for ideal science, that is, for science as we do not have it—as yet and perhaps never will?

To be sure, "influential" certainly does not *mean* "important." But, nevertheless, being influential is our best-available *test* for importance in science. Blue litmus paper turning red is certainly not what we *mean* by "acid," but it is nonetheless a pretty good indicator of acidity. Of course, what we need in such cases is a theory, an explanation for why the test standard (be it changing colors or influentiality) deserves to be seen as an indicator for the subject item (be it acidity or importance). Can such an account actually be provided in the present case of influence and importance? The answer is clearly yes. The crucial consideration here is that scientists are for the most part *rational* in matters relating to their work—indeed, the scientific community is perhaps our best-available paradigm of the rational society. It is a key consequence of this rationality that a thesis or theory just would not belong to actual science if it were not part of our best-available estimate of what belongs to ideal science. And, conversely, when an issue does belong to our very best estimate of an issue of science, its practitioners are bound to give it credence.

This stance of seeing the actual as a surrogate for the ideal is, of course, of limited applicability. In fields other than science—the humanities for one—we cannot presume a correlation between attention and importance. Take philosophy and even the philosophy of science—indeed, take as an instance this very issue we are considering: importance. Surely, this is not an unimportant topic, and yet as we saw at the very outset it is one that has engendered only a miniscule literature.

What is at issue here is an aspect of functionalistic pragmatism. The point is that science is a particular sort of enterprise with a particular goal structure. It aims both at the description and explanation of natural phenomena and (no less importantly) of the sort of control over nature that we are able to achieve in experiential situations and in technological applications. Science is not just chit-chat. The inherent teleology of the praxis at issue here provides for a goal-oriented, discourse-independent reality control geared to applicative efficacy. Accordingly, the importance of scientific findings is, in the final analysis, a matter of their utility within the discipline itself. And it is just this consideration that underlies the principle that citation prominence affords a plausible estimate of importance. For citations reflect use, and use is our best-available index of the cognitive usefulness that, in the present context, is the hallmark of importance.

So we return to the basics. Cognitive importance, like the idea of scientific truth on which it pivots, is by nature a decidedly idealized conception. And in this imperfectly mundane dispensation of ours we have no access to the ideal. In matters of science, too, we have no alternative but to let the best estimate that we can get make do provisionally as a placeholder for the best there is. And just this is the case with even so important an idea as that of importance.

Conclusion

The importance of a scientific idea or thesis is, in the end, a matter of its role in maintaining the overall harmony of our body of knowledge. After all, the maintenance of appropriate proportions is one of the definitive features in harmony. And this is as true in matters of cognition as elsewhere. In the pursuit of knowledge and in its organization, cultivating harmony through proper balance and proportion is a critical desideratum. The resources that the scientific community allocates to various problems and problem areas is a crucial factor here. And this holds not just for discussion space. The overall investment that our universities and research institutions devote to investigating in the issue involved—the amount of shelf space our libraries dedicate to the discussion of relevant matters—reflects a proportionality with putative importance. In all of these aspects of cognitive endeavor it is critical that resources be allocated with a view to the importance of the issues. And with this proportioning, as elsewhere, the cultivation of cognitive harmony is an indispensable requisite for the rational cogency of our proceedings.[10]

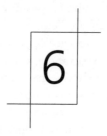

Why Philosophy Itself Must Be Systemically Harmonious

Externalities and Negative Side Effects

In no sector of cognitive theorizing does the concept of epistemic harmonization play a more crucial role than in philosophy. It is illuminating to approach this issue from an economic perspective. Economists characterize as "externalities" the costs that a given agent's operations engender for other participants in the economic system—the expenditures that one agent's activities exact from other agents, whether willingly or unwillingly. These are the operating costs that an agent simply off-loads onto the wider community: the expenses that one generates for others in the course of addressing one's own immediate concerns—as, for example, when a farmer's fertilizers contaminate the drinking water of his neighbors. It is interesting to observe that substantially the same phenomenon can also arise in philosophy. For in philosophy we may, in solving a problem within some particular domain, create major difficulties for the solution of problems elsewhere, even in areas seemingly far removed from the original issue. It is instructive to consider some examples of this phenomenon.

Example 1: Epistemology and Ethics

Suppose we are at sea vacationing on a cruise ship. It is dusk, and visibility is poor. As we stroll along the deck of the ship, someone suddenly shouts, "Man overboard!" Someone near us grabs a life preserver from the nearby bulkhead and rushes with it toward the railing. But then this person hesitates, and to our astonishment he calmly turns, retraces his steps, and replaces the life preserver back on the bulkhead as the ship moves past the region of the incident, first out of reach, then out of sight. Puzzled and chagrined, we turn to this person and ask why he aborted the rescue attempt. His response runs as follows: "Of course, throwing that life preserver was my first inclination, as my behavior clearly showed. But then some ideas from my undergraduate epistemology courses came to mind and convinced me that it made no sense to continue." Intrigued, we ask for more details and receive the following response:

> Consider what we actually knew. All we could see was that something that looked like a human head was bobbing out there in the water. But the visibility was poor. It could have been an old mop or a lady's wig stand. Those noises we took for distant shouts would well have been no more than a pulsing of the engines and the howling of the wind. There was simply no decisive evidence that it was actually a person out there. And then I remembered William Kingdon Clifford's classic dictum: "It is wrong always, everywhere, and for anyone, to believe anything upon insufficient evidence." So why act on a belief that there was actually a human being in danger out there, when the evidence for any such belief was clearly insufficient? And why carry out a rescue attempt when you do not accept that someone actually needs rescuing?

Something has clearly gone wrong here. We may choose not to fault our misguided shipmate for being an epistemologist, but we have to wonder about his moral competency.

Even if I unhesitatingly accept and endorse the abstract principle that one must try to be helpful to others in situations of need, I am clearly in moral difficulty if I operate on too stringent a standard of evidence in relevant contexts—if, for example, I allow skeptical concerns about others' minds to paralyze me from ever recognizing another creature as a human being. For then I will be far-reachingly precluded from doing things that, morally considered, I *ought* to do. William James rightly noted this connection between epistemology and morality, in insisting that the skeptic rudely treads on morality underfoot: "If I refuse to stop a murder because I am in [some] doubt whether it is not justifiable homicide, I am virtually abetting the crime. If I refuse to bale out a boat because I am in doubt whether my effort will keep her afloat, I am really helping to sink her. . . . Skepticism in moral matters is an active ally of immorality."[1] There is much to be said for this view of the matter.

To operate in life with *epistemological* principles so stringent as to impede the discharge of one's standard *moral* obligations is to invite justified reproach. Where the interests of others are at risk, we cannot, with moral appropriateness, deploy evidential standards of acceptability of a higher, more demanding sort than those that are normally operative in the community in the ordinary run of cases. At this point, epistemology has moral ramifications. For morality as we know it requires a commonsense, down-to-earth epistemology for its appropriate implementation.

In such a case, then, the stance we take in the one domain (epistemology) has significant repercussions for the way we can proceed in the other (ethics). The issues arising in these seemingly remote areas stand in systemic interlinkage. Externalities can come into play. A problem solution that looks like a bargain in one domain may exact an unacceptable price in another.

Example 2: Semantics and Metaphysics

For another illustration—one of a rather different sort—consider the semantical position urged by a contemporary Oxford philosopher who maintains that there are no incognizable facts, because there actually is a fact of the matter only when a claim to this effect is such

that "we [humans] could in a finite time bring ourselves into a position in which we were [fully] justified either in asserting or in denying
[the contention at issue]."[2] This sort of "finite decidability semantics"
holds that a proposition is communicatively meaningful—qualifies as
inherently true or false—only if the matter can actually be settled, decisively and conclusively, one way or the other, by a finite effort in a
limited time.

But this doctrinal path issuing from semantics leads to some
strange destinations. For it automatically precludes the prospect of
maintaining anything like our commonsense view of things in the
world about us. In this way, the wolf of a highly problematic meta-
physic comes concealed in the sheep's clothing of innocuous-looking
semantical theory. Consider that as we conventionally think about
things within the conceptual framework of our fact-oriented thought
and discourse, *any* real physical object has more facets than it will or
indeed can ever actually manifest in experience. Every objective prop-
erty of a real thing has consequences of a dispositional nature, and
these are never actually surveyable in toto, seeing that the dispositions
that particular concrete things inevitably have endow them with an in-
finitistic aspect that cannot be comprehended within experience. A
desk, for example, has a limitless manifold of phenomenal features of
the type "having a certain appearance from a particular point of view."
It is perfectly clear that most of these will never be actualized in experience. Moreover, a thing *is* what it *does:* to be a desk or an apple is to
behave like one. Entity and lawfulness are coordinated correlates—a
good Kantian point.[3] And this fact, that things as such involve lawful
comportment, means that the finitude of experience precludes any
prospect of the *exhaustive* manifestation of the descriptive facets of
any real thing.

A real thing is always conceptualized as having features that transcend our actual experience of it. All discourse about objective things
involves an element of *experience-transcending imputation*—of commitment to claims that go beyond the experientially acquirable information, yet claims whose rejection would mean our having to with-
draw the characterization of the thing at issue. To say of something
that it is an apple or a stone or a tree is to become inexorably com-

mitted to claims about it that go beyond the data we have—and even beyond those that we can, in the nature of things, ever actually acquire. Real things always do and must have features that transcend our determinable knowledge of them.

In light of such considerations, it emerges that a finite decidability semantics—though seemingly a merely linguistic doctrine about meaningful assertion—is by no means just theory of language or logic. For it now has major repercussions in very different domains. In particular, it has the far-reaching metaphysical consequence of precluding any prospect of the commonsense realism at issue in our standard conception of the world's things. On its basis, any statement of objective fact—however modest and pedestrian—is immediately rendered meaningless by the infinitude of its evidential ramifications. Thus, a "merely semantical" doctrine seemingly devised to serve the interests of a philosophy of language has implications that preempt a major substantive position in metaphysics.

Its conflict with the commonsense realism of ordinary discourse does not, of course, demonstrate that finite decidability semantics is ultimately incorrect. But it once again illustrates vividly the ramified interconnectedness of philosophical doctrines—the fact that a seemingly attractive problem solution in one area may be available as such only at the cost of creating massive problems elsewhere. The theory is certainly one that we cannot reasonably accept on its local, semantical recommendations alone, irrespective of wider implications. Externalities are once again at work.

And further illustrations are readily available. A metaphysical determinism that negates free will runs afoul of a traditionalistic ethical theory that presupposes it. A philosophical anthropology that takes human life to originate at conception clashes with a social philosophy that sees abortion as morally unproblematic. A theory of rights that locates all responsibility in the contractual reciprocity of freely consenting parties creates problems for a morality of concern for animals. And the list goes on and on. For the systemic integrity of the discipline renders unacceptable the disharmony among the doctrines of its several subdomains that all too readily arise in the absence of due care for larger interrelationships.

Systematic Interconnectedness as a Consequence of Aporetic Complexity

The examples we have been considering convey a clear lesson. Philosophical doctrines are inextricably interconnected, spreading their implications across the frontiers of very different and seemingly disparate areas. The ramifications and implications of philosophical contentions do not respect a discipline's taxonomic boundaries. And we all too easily risk losing sight of this interconnectedness when we pursue the technicalities of a narrow subdomain. In actuality, the stance we take on questions in one domain will generally have substantial implications and ramification for very different issues in other, seemingly unrelated domains. And this is exactly why systematization is so important in philosophy—because the way we *do* answer some questions will have limiting repercussions for the way we *can* answer others. We cannot emplace our philosophical convictions into conveniently delineated compartments in the comfortable expectation that what we maintain in one area of the field will have no unwelcome implications for what we are inclined to maintain in others.

And so in philosophy, too, the realm of truth—or putative truth—is unified, and its components are interlinked. Change your mind, change one fact about the real, and all the rest is affected. To qualify as adequate, one's account of things must be a systemic whole whose components are interrelated through systemic interaction or feedback. In the final analysis, philosophy is a system because it is concerned with indicating, or at least with *estimating*, the truth about things, and "the truth about reality" is a system. Its various sectors and components are bound to dovetail smoothly with one another. Even if one were reluctant to claim that *reality* as such must be systematic, the fact remains that an adequate *account* of it must surely be so. Even as we must take a sober view of inebriation, so we must aim at a coherent account of even an incoherent world. Philosophy's commitment to the project of rational inquiry, to the task of making coherent and comprehensive sense of things, means that an adequate philosophy must be holistic, accommodating and coordinating all aspects of its concerns in a single unified and coherent whole, with the result that any viable philosophical doctrine will and can be no more than a particular piece fitting smoothly into a puzzle.

After all, in philosophy there are no secure axioms, there is no starter set of absolutely certain "givens" whose implications we can follow without question to the bitter end. In general, we cannot assess the acceptability of our contentions solely in terms of the security of their antecedents; instead, we must reassess their acceptability in light of their consequences, not only locally but also globally. The implicit interconnectedness of philosophical issues means that the price philosophers must pay for overly narrow specialization—for confining attention narrowly to one particular set of issues—is compromising the tenability of their positions.

Insofar as such a perspective is correct, it emerges that the range of relevant consequences cannot be confined to the local area of the immediate thematic environs of the contention but will have to involve its more remote reverberations as well. If an otherwise appealing contention in semantics wreaks havoc in metaphysics or in the philosophy of mathematics, that, too, will have to be weighed when the question of its tenability arises. The absolute idealist for whom "time is unreal" cannot appropriately just write off the ethicist's interest in future eventuations (as regards, for example, the situation that will obtain when the time to make good a promise arrives)—or the political philosopher's concern for the well-being of future generations. The materialist cannot simply dismiss the boundary-line issues involved in the moral question of why pointlessly damaging a computer one owns is simply foolish, but pointlessly injuring an animal is actually wicked. The long and short of it is that philosophical issues are organically interconnected. Positions that maximize local advantages may fail to be optimal from a global point of view. In the final analysis, only positions that are *holistically* adequate through a concern for synoptic harmony can be deemed to be really satisfactory.

From Greek antiquity to the nineteenth century, a conviction prevailed that the branches of philosophy could be arranged in a neat hierarchy of sequential dependence and fundamentality, somewhat along the lines of logic, epistemology, metaphysics, ethics (axiology), and politicosocial philosophy. In fact, however, the various subdo-

mains of philosophy are interlinked by a complex network of reciprocal interrelationships. (For example, one needs epistemology to validate principles of logic, and one must use logic for reasoning in epistemology.) Justificatory argumentation in philosophy admits of no
neat Aristotelian order of priority/posteriority in its involvement with
the subject's components. The inherent interrelationships of the issues
are such that we have no alternative but to see the sectors of philosophy as interconnected in interlocking cycles that bind the subject's various branches into one systematic whole.

Because its issues are interrelated, philosophical argumentation
must look not just to antecedents but to consequences as well. Virtually nothing of philosophical relevancy is beyond question or altogether immune to criticism and possible rejection. Pretty much everything is potentially at risk. All of the "data" of philosophy are
defeasible—anything might in the final analysis have to be abandoned, whatever its source: science, common sense, common knowledge. One recent theorist writes: "No philosophical, or any other, theory can provide a view which violates common sense and remain
logically consistent. For the truth of common sense is assumed by all
theories. . . . This necessity to conform to common sense establishes a
constraint upon the interpretations philosophical theories can offer."[4]
But this overstates the case. The philosophical landscape is littered
with theories that tread common sense underfoot. As philosophy goes
about its work of rendering our beliefs coherent, something to which
we are deeply attached often has to give somewhere along the line, and
we can never say at the outset where the chips will or will not fall. Systemic considerations may well in the end lead our most solid-seeming
suppositions into insuperable difficulty—even as can happen in the
context of natural science. And the only cure for failures of systematization in philosophy lies in the construction of better, more harmon-
ic systems.

Local Minimalism versus Global Optimalism

In philosophy, as in various other cognitive domains, two very different approaches to problem solving can be implemented. The first is

the narrow, localist course of opting for the least risky—and thus the least informative—answer to our immediate questions that can accommodate the putative facts of the case (minimalism). The second is the more ambitious course of opting for the globally most adequate—and thus most risky—answer among the "available" answers that are compatible with the facts (maximalism).

Confronted with this choice, the epistemic localist is a pessimist who opts for the first, more modest option. The epistemic globalist, on the other hand, is an optimist who opts for the second, more ambitious alternative. For the localist, what matters is the least costly solution to the range of problems that lie immediately at hand. With Occam's razor as his favored instrument, he rejects out of hand any entities, concepts, or theses that do not answer to the requirements of immediate needs. A global approach, by contrast, looks beyond the issues of the moment toward those that will predictably arise further down the road. The global maximalist wants tools that are serviceable not only for the immediate problem situation but also for the wider issues that seem likely to arise. In dealing with immediate concerns the maximalist keeps a weather eye on more distant horizons. Globalists are constantly mindful of the big picture. With them, the impetus to systematizing is paramount, and ingenuity enjoins epistemic optimism.

Localists buy a hammer just big enough to drive in the nails they have on hand. They see the prospect of the larger nails they may be handling tomorrow as immaterial—something to be dealt with if and when the time comes. When they marry, localists buy houses just large enough for themselves and their spouses. The idea that, for a modest additional expenditure, they can buy a larger house also adequate to their needs if and when children arrive does not move them. They are penny wise and pound foolish; for them, finding the cheapest solution to the immediate problem is all that counts. They do not consider the idea of expending resources to provide extra capacity and spare power for the future.

Proceeding in this spirit, various schools of epistemic minimalism go about posting signposts that put all risk of engaging larger issues *off limits*. Such theorists turn Occam's razor into Robespierre's guillotine. Their tumbrels carry off a wide variety of victims:

- *Sets* in the philosophy of mathematics
- *Abstracta* in semantics
- *Unobservable entities* in the philosophy of physics
- *Dispositional theses* in the philosophy of language
- *Obligations* that reach beyond the requisites of prudence in moral theory, and so on.

Reluctant to venture beyond the immediate, local, case-specific requisites of the first-order agenda of epistemological demands, the philosophical minimalist is content to accept incomprehension on the larger issues. All too often, observability alone is the minimalist's standard of reality, and causal and explanatory questions are ruled out. Why do phenomena have the character we observe? Don't ask. What accounts for the lawfulness of their interrelationships? Don't ask! Why are they uniform for different observers? Don't ask! What of factual claims that go beyond observability? Throw them out! What about claims that transcend the prospect of decisive verification? Throw them out, too!

But such an approach is not without its problems. The fact is that, in philosophy, as elsewhere, localistic minimalism proves to be a very questionable bargain. Here, as elsewhere, some investment in added capacity is generally required for extra capability. In philosophy, as in life, the economies of a localistic minimalism are unwise practices that frequently produce long-term waste.

The systematic nature of philosophy-as-a-whole has far-reaching implications for the proper cultivation of the discipline. In particular, it means that we should not—nay, cannot—rest satisfied with isolated piecework, with single bits of doctrine whose merits do not extend beyond immediate adequacy in a local problem area. For in philosophizing, as in economic matters, externalities may come into play. A seemingly elegant solution to the difficulties posed by one problem may carry in its wake hopeless difficulties for the satisfactory resolution of some other problem. Its ramifications in another, seemingly remote area may require one to pay an unacceptable price for the neat resolution of a problem in a given domain. One may, as we have seen, be forced into accepting an epistemology that one does not much like for itself in the interests of possibilizing an ethical position that one deems essential.

Philosophizing is, in this regard, akin to cognitive engineering, for the sensible philosopher, like the sensible engineer, must proceed holistically with a view to the *overall* implications of his or her particular ventures in problem solving. Engineers who allow one particular desideratum (cost, safety, fuel economy, repair infrequency, or the like) to dominate their thinking, to the exclusion of all else, would produce not a viable product but an absurdity. We would certainly laugh at someone who offered to build us a super-safe car that could only go two miles an hour. Surely, a similar derision is deserved by the skeptic who offers to build us a super-safe, error-excluding epistemology that would not, however, allow us to maintain a line of distinction between science and pseudoscience. In philosophy as in economics, engineering, and medicine we cannot avoid concern for externalities and have to come to grips with incidental interactions and side effects. In chess, we cannot play rooks independently of what we do with bishops; in medicine, we cannot treat one organ without considering the implications for others; in political economy, we cannot design policies for one sector without concerning ourselves with their impact on the rest. In most any problem-solving contexts we do well to keep all our commitments in reasonable coordination overall. Why should philosophy be any different?

A philosopher who achieves his or her proximate, localized ends at the cost of off-loading difficulties onto other sectors of the wider domain is simply not doing an adequate job. With rationally cogent philosophizing, it is not local minimalism but global optimalism that is required. To be acceptable, a philosophical problem solution must form an integral part of a wider doctrine that makes acceptably good sense overall. Here only, systemic, holistically attuned positions can yield truly satisfactory solutions—solutions that do not involve undue externalities for the larger scheme of things. For better or for worse, viable philosophizing has to be a matter of holistic systematization. Tenable philosophy must be a systematically dovetailed whole. For in the end the range of our philosophical concern is a network where everything is systematically interconnected with everything else. A tenable philosophy must be a harmoniously dovetailed whole.[5]

The Imperative of Cognitive Rationality

The pursuit of the harmonious integrity of rational coherence among our question-answering commitments—their consistency, compatibility, comprehensiveness—is crucial for philosophical method. But are there facts to justify this emphasis on order and logical tidiness? Is it really necessary to proceed on this basis? Are systematic coherence and consistency themselves not simply the hobgoblins of small minds? Is systematicity coherence itself not a mere ornament, a dispensable luxury?

When Alice was in Wonderland, she insisted that "one can't believe impossible things." The White Queen replied: "I daresay you haven't had much practice. When I was your age, I always did it for half-an-hour a day. Why, sometimes I've believed as many as six impossible things before breakfast." Yet, even with practice, this task is uncomfortable and unsatisfying. A profound commitment to the demands of rationality is a thread that runs through the whole fabric of our philosophizing; the dedication to consistency is the most fundamental imperative of reason. "Keep your commitments consistent" is philosophy's ruling injunction. We do not want just answers, but reasoned answers, defensible answers that square with what we are going to say in other contexts and on other occasions. And this means that we must go back and clean out the Augean stable of our cognitive inclinations, seeing that the commitment to rational coherence is a part of what makes philosophy the enterprise it is.

After all, to endorse a discordant diversity of claims is in the end not to enrich one's position through a particularly generous policy of acceptance but to impoverish it. To accept both p and not-p is effectively to have nothing at all. To refuse to discriminate is to go empty handed, without answers to our questions. It is not a particularly elevated way of doing philosophy but a way of not doing philosophy at all. For it evades the problems of the field, abandoning the traditional project of philosophy as rational problem solving. We are compelled to systematize our knowledge into a coherent whole by regimenting what we accept in light of principles of rationality. Philosophizing is a work of reason; we want our problem resolutions to be backed by good reasons—reasons whose bearing will doubtless not be absolute and definitive but will, at any rate, be as compelling as is possible in the circumstances. Reasoning and argumentation are thus the lifeblood of philosophy. Here, as is the case throughout the domain of rational inquiry, if we do not have a doctrine that is consistent and coherent, then we have nothing.

Of course, no rationally stringent guarantee can be issued in advance—prior to any furtherance of the enterprise itself—no categorical assurance given that our philosophical efforts at systematizing our knowledge of the world are bound to succeed. The systematicity of our knowledge is (as we shall see) not something that can be guaranteed a priori as having to obtain on the basis of the "general principles" of the matter. The parameters of harmonious systematicity—coherence, consistency, uniformity, and the rest—are methodological guides. They represent a family of *regulative ideals* toward whose realization our cognitive endeavors do and should strive. But this drive for systematicity is the operative expression of a governing ideal and not something whose realization can be taken for granted as already certain and settled from the very outset. The extent to which our efforts at philosophizing manage to succeed in achieving the objectives at issue is always "something that remains to be seen"—a circumstance that, in *this* regard, replicates exactly the situation of natural science.

The proof of the pudding lies in the eating. We set out from the consideration that a satisfactory philosophy must be systematic: that *if* a satisfying philosophy is to be realized, *then* it will have to be one that is systematic. We are dealing here with a condition of adequacy. Only time and effort can ultimately tell whether this goal is actually achieved. The justification of systematicity as a regulative ideal for our philosophy must thus be seen in essentially instrumental terms. "Conduct your cognitive proceedings with a view to the pursuit of systematicity!" is a regulative principle of inquiry whose legitimation ultimately lies in its pragmatic utility with respect to the teleology of the project at issue. Our commitment in philosophy to the pursuit of harmonious systematicity is justified by the consideration that it provides the only effective route to achieving the characterizing aims of the enterprise.

It must be emphasized that the impetus toward rational coherence does not in any way prejudge the *outcome* of our theorizing. It may well turn out in the end that the "principle of noncontradiction" does not hold for the world; reality as best as we can discern it may turn out to be inconsistent. But what is presently at issue is not reality as such but our *account* of it. Regardless of the world's consistency, our *theory* of it must be self-consistent if it is to merit serious consideration. And here it is important to recognize that thought need not necessarily share the features of its object. A sober study of inebriation is perfectly possible, as is a coherent characterization of the opinions of an incoherent thinker or a consistent characterization of an inconsistent system (where we insert another assertion—perhaps "the nature of things"—between ourselves and those "inconsistent facts"). A coherent theory of an inconsistent reality can perfectly well be contemplated.[6] A methodological insistence on consistency does not prejudge the ontological nature of the real; what is at issue is simply the consistency and coherence of our own deliberations. We might in the end be driven by considerations of rationality itself to the conclusion that reality is inconsistent, but this is no reason to cease striving for consistency in our *theory* of reality—at any rate, until such time as a clear demonstration of the actual impossibility of reaching this goal becomes available.

The Methodological Rationale of Systematic Harmony in Philosophy

The preceding discussion has emphasized that the deliberative work of philosophy needs to be accomplished systematically—that in the interests of adequacy, philosophizing must aim at a system that is at once comprehensive in its purview and harmonious in its articulation. But does this requirement not prejudice the substantive issues— does it not precommit us to the view that the world is a system? After all, any such presupposition or presumption would clearly be inappropriate in philosophy. This is an issue that needs to be addressed.

The materials for a resolution are already in hand. For, as was noted above, the conception of a system has historically been applied both to *things* in the world and to *bodies of knowledge,* and it is accordingly important to distinguish between the *ontological* systematicity (simplicity, coherence, regularity, uniformity) of the *objects* of our knowledge—that is, between systematicity as a feature characterizing the manifold of existing things—and the *cognitive* systematicity of our (putative) knowledge of *information* regarding such things. And the fact of it is that the cognitive parameters at issue in systematic harmony—simplicity, regularity, coherence, unity, uniformity, and the rest—have the standing of regulative principles of probative procedure. They implement the idea of epistemic preferability or precedence, of presumption and burden of proof, by indicating where, in the absence of specific counterindications, our epistemic commitments are to be placed in weaving together the fabric of our knowledge. Such a procedural/methodological stance does not anticipate and prejudge the ultimate answer to the questions we pose about the harmonious makeup of the real. All that it does is to guide and control the process by which the answers—whatever they may be—are attained. No substantive issues are prejudged by the methodological commitment to harmonious systematicity that is crucial to the process of rational inquiry on which philosophy is engaged. All in all, then, the idea of harmonization is destined to play a pivotal role not only in our philosophical doctrines but also in our manner of philosophizing.

Notes

CHAPTER 1: THE SYSTEMIC HARMONY OF FACT

1. See *harmonia* in H. G. Liddell and R. Scott, *A Greek-English Lexicon*, 7th ed. (Oxford: Oxford University Press, 1959).

2. André Lalande's *Vocabulaire technique et critique de le philosophie* (6th ed., Paris: Presses Univeritaires de France, 1988) defends *harmony* in its general sense as *"unité organique d'une multiplicité,"* and speaks of *"une combination heureuse d'éléments diverses"* (401). It proceeds to cite an author who insists that *"toute harmonie implique une charactère esthétique,"* but it is clear that the positivity at issue with "harmonious functioning" need not be sensuous but could be intellectual or even moral." (When we say that "the negotiations achieved a harmonious accommodation in resolving the conflict," there need be nothing particularly aesthetic about it.)

3. The pre-Socratic philosopher Heraclitus of Ephesos held that uniting the tension of opposed forces—as with the bow and its bowstring or the lyre and its string—represents the quintessence of harmony.

4. Compare the closely analogous definition given by Anatol Rapoport in "Systems Analysis: I. General Systems Theory," in the *International Encyclopedia of the Social Sciences*, vol. 15 (New York: Macmillan, 1968), 452–56.

5. Translated in part in N. Kretzmann and E. Stump, *The Cambridge Translation of Medieval Philosophical Texts*, vol. 1, *Logic and Philosophy of Language* (Cambridge: Cambridge University Press, 1988), 389–412.

6. The main theoretical works are various essays by Lambert (including the opuscula "Fragment einer Systematologie" (with parts dated 1767 and 1771), "Theorie des Systems" (1782), and "Von den Lücken unserer Erkenntniss" (ca. 1785); and, of course, Kant's *Critique of Pure Reason* (1781), especially bk. 2, pt. 3, "The Architectonic of Pure Reason." Lambert's philosophical writings were issued by J. Bernouili, ed., *Johann Henrich Lambert: Logische und Philosophische Abhandlungen*, 2 vols. (Berlin, 1782 and 1787; reprinted Hildesheim, 1967, ed. H. W. Arndt).

7. See chapter 7 of Nicholas Rescher, *The Coherence Theory of Truth* (Oxford: Basil Blackwell, 1973), for further discussion of some of the relevant issues.

8. A cognitive system is never "merely descriptive"—any scientific scheme of classification always proceeds in line with *explanatory* considerations.

9. For a useful general treatment of planning theory see G. A. Miller, E. Galanter, and K. H. Pribram, *Plans and the Structure of Behavior* (New York: Holt, 1960). The parallelism of planning and systematizing was stressed by Hugo Dingler. See his *Das System* (München: E. Reinhardt, 1930), 127ff.

10. See Christopher Alexander, *Notes on the Synthesis of Form* (Cambridge, MA: Harvard University Press, 1964).

11. Compare Robert Ardrey, *Hunting Hypothesis* (New York: Atheneum, 1976).

12. *Logic*, sect. 889; cited in Theodore Ziehen, *Lehrbuch der logik* (Bonn: A. Marcus & E. Webers Verlag, 1920), 821.

13. Elsewhere Plato speaks of this arrangement as "divine harmony" (*theia harmonia*): *Timaeus*, 80B.

14. The economic contrast between maximizing and satisficing affords an instructive analogy here.

15. As J. H. Lambert puts it, the parts of a system should *"alle mit einander so vervunden sein, dass sie gerade das der vorgesetzten Absicht gemässe Ganze ausmachen."* Quoted in Otto Ritschl, *System and systematishce Methode in der Geshichte des wissenschaftlichen Sprachgebrauchs und der philosophischen Methodologie* (Bonn, 1906), 64.

CHAPTER 2: COGNITIVE HARMONY IN HISTORICAL PERSPECTIVE

1. Thus De Cange, *Glossarium mediae et infimae latinatatis* (Paris, 1842): *Systema, proprie compages, collectio. Hinc astronomis pro mundi constitutione et forma usurpatur. Theologis vero pro complexu articulorum fidei.* The term gradually drove its rival *syntagma* from the field in this latter sense.

2. Thus, Bartholomaeus Keckerman (d. 1609) wrote in his treatise *Systema logicae tribus libris adornatum* (Hanover, 1600) that what is at issue is the whole organized body of logical precepts. He explained that the term *logic*, like that for every other art, stands for two things: on the one hand, it refers to the practical skill (*habitus*), on the other, to systematic discipline: *primo pro habitu ipso in mentem per praecceptu et exercitationem introducto: deide pro praecptorium logicorum comprehensione seu systemate.* Quoted in Ritschl, *System*, 27. Keckerman's later (1606) handbook of logic appeared under the title *Systema Minus*. His contemporary Clemens Timpler (d. ca. 1625) wrote in his *Metaphysicae Systema Methodicum* (Hanover, 1606) that in an exposition that is ordered and structured according to proper methodological principles, *systema non confusum et pertubatum, sed bene secundum leges methodi ordinatum et dispositum.*

3. More than 130 titles of this sort published during the seventeenth century are listed in Ritschl, *System*. Some examples are Johann Heinrich Alsted, *Systema mnemonicum duplex* (Frankfurt, 1610); Nicas de Fevrue, *Systema chymicum*

(Paris, 1666, in French; London, 1966, in English), Richard Elton, *Systema atis militaris* (London, 1669). For details, see Ritschl, *System.*

4. There is no entry for *system* in the *Lexicon Philosophicum* of Rudolf Goclenius (Frankfurt, 1623). But in that of Johann Micraelius (Stettin, 1653) the term is explained in its literary sense as a systematic exposition.

5. Thus Leibniz contrasts his own *système de l'harmonie préétablie* with the *système des causes efficientes et celui des causes finales* as well as the *système des causes occasionelles qui a été fort mis en vogue par les belles réflexions de l'Auteur de la Recherche de la Vérté* (Malebranche). He characterizes his own contribution as the *système nouveau de la nature et de la communication des substances aussi bien que de l'union qu'il y a entre l'âme et le corps.* Ritschl, *System,* 60.

6. See his *Traité des systèmes* first published in Paris in 1749.

7. Most writers about systems have recognized and indeed stressed this duality. See, for example, Hugo Dingler, *Das System* (Munich: Zeiss, 1930), 128ff.

8. Much of the presently surveyed information regarding the history of the term is drawn from Ritschl, *System.* Further data are given in the review of Ritschl's work by August Messer in the *Göttinger gelehrte Anzeigen* 169, no. 8 (1907). See also Aloys von der Stein, "Der Systembegriff in seiner geschichtlichen Entwicklung," in *System und Klassifikation in Wissenschaft und Dokumentation,* ed. Aloys Diemer (Meisenheim am Glan: A. Hain, 1968).

9. See Theodor Ziehen, *Lehrbuch der Logic* (Bonn: A Marcus & E. Weber Verlag, 1920), 821. The foundation of the Stoic's approaches lies in Aristotle's *De mundo.* But contrast Sextus Empiricus, *Outline of Pyrrhonism,* III:269, which speaks of the *systéma* (collectivity) of the propositions of a syllogism.

10. The following passage is particularly apposite here: "The thing that can be thought and that for the sake of which the thought exists is one and the same; for you cannot find thought without also finding what it is uttered to be. And there is not, and never shall be, anything besides what is, since fate has chained it so as to be whole and immovable. . . . Since, then, it has a furthest limit, it is complete on every side, like the mass of rounded sphere, equally poised from the centre in every direction; for it cannot be greater or smaller in one place than in another. For there is nothing that could keep it from reaching out equally, nor can aught that is be more here and less there than it is, since it is all inviolable. For the point from which it is equal in every direction tends equally to the limits. Here shall I close my trustworthy speech and thought about the truth" (Frag. 8, Diels; trans. J. Burnet).

11. The system concept is operative with respect to knowledge at two distinguishable levels: the level of *propositions* (theses, theories, doctrines) and the level of *concepts* (conceptions, ideas). The present discussion will focus on the former. Conceptual systems are, after all, embedded in thesis systems: our concepts are defined, specified, determined, and explained in terms of the theses in which they figure. The systematization of our concepts and categories is accordingly su-

pervenient upon that of the propositional systems in which these concepts and categories play their characteristic role.

12. Immanuel Kant, *Critique of Pure Reason,* trans. Norman Kemp Smith (New York, St. Martin's Press, 1963), A833, B861. Seen in this light, Herman Lotze's dictum that human thought never does and never can rest until "the whole context of reality is conceived under some principle of organic unity" can be seen in a more prosaic light as indicating human insistence on achieving scientific knowledge of the environing world.

13. Kant, *Critique,* A834, B862.

14. In view of this fact, it is strange that so little attention has been paid to cognitive ("intellectual," "symbolic") systems within the recent general systems theory movement. Thus, in Ludwig von Bertalanffy's synoptic survey *General Systems Theory: Foundations, Development, Applications* (New York, 1968), the distinction is recognized, but without any elaboration or discussion of issues on the cognitive side.

15. Richard S. Rudner, *Philosophy of Social Science* (Englewood Cliffs, NJ.: Prentice Hall, 1966), 89.

16. In an interesting recent article, "On the Concept of a System," *Philosophy of Science* 42 (1975): 448–68, J. H. Marchall reaches a precisely parallel conclusion on the basis of an examination of systems discourse emanating from the general systems theory movement.

17. "Fragment einer Systematologie," 386.

18. Kant, *Critique,* A832, B860.

19. The idea that in explicating the notion of a "law of nature" we shall take systematicity as our standard of lawfulness was a standard among the English neo-Hegelians. It recurs in F. P. Ramsey, who in an unpublished note of 1928 proposed to characterize laws as the "consequence of those propositions which we should take as axioms if we knew everything and organized it as simply as possible in a deductive system"; see David Lewis, *Counterfactuals* (Cambridge, MA: Harvard University Press, 1973), 73. Ramsey gives the theory an interesting—but in principle gratuitous—twist in the direction of a specifically *deductive* style of systematization, a specification the Hegelians had made along coherentist rather than deductivist lines. The more orthodoxly neo-Hegelian, coherentist version of the theory was refurbished in the author's *Scientific Explanation* (New York: Free Press, 1971 see especially 1110–111). Parts of the present discussion draw on this work.

20. St. Thomas Aquinas also wrote that an "architect" was a man who knew how things should be ordered and arranged, and that the word could be more appropriately applied to a philosopher than to a builder. Quoted in Paul Frankl, *The Gothic: Literary Sources and Interpretations* (Princeton, NJ: Princeton University Press, 1960), 135.

21. Kant, *Critique,* A832, B860. Compare "Every discipline (*Lehre*) if it be a system—that is, a cognitive whole ordered according to principles—is called a science," Immanuel Kant, preface to *The Metaphysical Foundation of Natural Science* (trans. L. W. Beck).

22. Kant, *Critique,* A834, B862.

23. Kant, *Critique,* A834, B862.

24. Karl Pearson, *The Grammar of Science* (London: A. and C. Black, 1900), chap. 1, sec. 14.

25. *Palintropos harmoninê hokôsper toxou kai lyrês,* G. S. Kirk, J. T. Raven, and M. Schofield, *The Presocratic Philosophers* (Cambridge: University of Cambridge Press, 1983), sec. 209.

26. To De Volder, July 6, 1701, in Leibniz's *Philosophishe Schriften,* ed. G. I. Gerhardt, vol. 2, 226 (Berlin: Weidmann, 1979), my translation.

27. "On Truth and Coherence," *Essays on Truth and Reality* (Oxford: Clarendon Press, 1914), 202–203, 210.

28. Introduction to Kant's *Critique of Judgment* in *Werke,* vol. 5, Academy edition (Berlin, 1920), 202.

29. However, it will emerge that the "knowledge agrees with reality" principle cannot be construed in such a way that the systematicity of our knowledge of reality guarantees that of reality itself. In this regard our present position parts company with the tradition.

30. Presumably, this is the cash value of the Hegelian view of explanation according to which "nothing can be known rightly, without knowing all else rightly"; Bernard Bosanquet, *Logic* (London: Macmillan, 1888), 393. If our system is to control our knowledge, then the system must be constructed antecedently so that such monitoring can be accomplished.

31. Brand Blanshard, *Reason and Analysis* (La Salle, IL: Open Court, 1962).

32. "'Absolute' and 'Relative' Truth," *Mind* 14 (1905), 9.

33. In his *Vocabulaire technique et critique de le philosophie,* André Lalande pointed out that talk of harmony is particularly prominent in recent French philosophy and singled out Felix Ravaisson for special mention in this regard.

CHAPTER 3: THE SYSTEMATICITY OF NATURE

1. The register of key thinkers who represented this included Pythagoras, Plato, and the Neoplatonists: Nicholas of Cusa, Paracelsus, Leibniz, and, more recently, Einstein.

2. Charles Sanders Peirce took the sensible line that the principles such as those of the uniformity or systematicity of nature represent not so much a substantive *claim* as an action-guiding *insinuation:* "Now you know how a malicious person who wishes to say something ill of another, prefers *insinuation,* that is, he speaks so vaguely that he suggests a great deal while he expressly says nothing at

all. In this way he avoids being confronted by the fact. It is the same with these principles of scientific inference. . . . They rather insinuate a uniformity than state it. And as insinuation always expresses the state of feeling of the person who uses it rather than anything in its object, so we may suppose these principles express rather the scientific attitude than a scientific result"; *Collected Papers,* vol. 7 (Cambridge, MA: Harvard University Press, 1931–1958), sec. 7.132.

3. Sanders Peirce, *Collected Papers,* vol. 7, sec. 7.219.

4. Reichenbach, *Experience and Prediction,* 376. Compare "Imagine that a physicist . . . wants to draw a curve which passes through [points on a graph that represent] the date observed. It is well known that the physicist chooses the simplest curve; this is not to be regarded as a matter of convenience [for different] curves correspond as to the measurements observed, but they differ as to future measurements; hence they signify different predictions based on the same observational material. The choice of the simplest curve, consequently, depends on an inductive assumption: we believe that the simplest curve gives the best predictions. . . . If in such cases the question of simplicity plays a certain role for our decision, it is because we make the assumptions that the simplest theory furnishes the best predictions." Reichenbach, *Experience and Prediction,* (Chicago: University of Chicago Press, 1938), 375–76.

5. See B. W. Petky, *The Fundamental Physical Constants and the Frontiers of Measurement* (Bristol: A. Hilger, 1985).

6. These considerations explain how we are to proceed in situations where the parameters of cognitive systematization stand in apparent conflict with one another, when conformity seems at odds with cohesiveness, or the like. Reconciliation is to be effected here in terms of the demands of overall economy.

7. Further considerations relevant to these issues are canvassed in Rescher, *Methodological Pragmatism* (Oxford: Basil Blackwell, 1977) and *Cognitive Systematization* (Oxford: Basil Blackwell, 1979).

CHAPTER 4: INDUCTIVE PRINCIPLES AS INSTRUMENTS
OF COGNITIVE HARMONIZATION

1. William Whewell, *Novum Organon Renovatum* (London: J. W. Parker and Son, 1858), 114.

2. The force of Dickinson Miller's principle must be acknowledged: "There is no intermediate degree between following from premises and not following from them. There is no such thing as half-following or quarter-following." Dickinson S. Miller, "Professor Donald Williams vs. Hume," *Journal of Philosophy* 44 (1947), 684.

3. This perspective supports F. H. Bradley in his critique of J. S. Mill's view of induction, on the basis of the consideration that inference as such is impotent to accomplish the move from particulars to universals because it is only legitimate to argue from some to all if it is premised that the particulars at issue share some universal character.

4. Carl G. Hempel, *Philosophy of Natural Science* (Englewood Cliffs, NJ: Prentice Hall, 1966), 15.

5. Henri Poincaré, *Science and Hypothesis* (New York: Scott, 1905), 145–46.

6. Galileo Galilei, *Dialogues Concerning Two New Sciences,* trans. H. Crew and A. de Salve (Evanston, IL: University of Illinois Press, 1914), 154.

7. Kant was the first philosopher clearly to perceive and emphasize this crucial point: "But such a principle [of systematicity] does not prescribe any law for objects; . . . it is merely a subjective law for the orderly management of the possessions of our understanding, that by the comparison of its concepts it may reduce them to the smallest possible number; it does not justify us in demanding from the objects such uniformity as will minister to the convenience and extension of our understanding; and we may not, therefore, ascribe to the [methodological or regulative] maxim [Systematize knowledge!] any objective [or descriptively constitutive] validity" (*Critique,* A306, B362). Compare also C. S. Peirce's contention that the systematicity of nature is a regulative matter of scientific attitude rather than a constitutive matter of scientific fact. Sanders Peirce, *Collected Papers,* vol. 7, 7.134.

8. Some issues revolving around this principle are discussed in Daniel Goldstick, "Methodological Conservatism," *American Philosophical Quarterly* 8 (1971): 186–91.

CHAPTER 5: HARMONY AND A SENSE OF PROPORTION
IN COGNITIVE EVALUATION

1. Karl R. Popper, *Conjectures and Refutations* (New York: Basic Books, 1962), 229.

2. Larry Laudan, *Progress and Its Problems* (Berkeley: University of California Press, 1971), 13.

3. Of course, one selfsame fact or theory may be important in one area of inquiry and unimportant in another and thus be important for one investigator's work but not for another's. But this issue-relative importance with regard to different problem contexts is different from importance per se from which "the larger scheme of things" becomes determinative.

4. It is of interest in this regard to recall F. P. Ramsey's suggestion that the laws of nature should be conceived of as the theories of the most economical axiomatization of a perfected science. F. P. Ramsey, *The Foundation of Mathematical and Other Logical Essays,* ed. R. B. Branthwaite (London: Routledge & Kegan Paul, 1931), 242. On this basis the laws will of course emerge as the most important findings of their respective branches of science because of the explanatory recourse to them—direct and indirect—will proliferate throughout the virtual exposition of the domain. And, of course, a change of laws will—according to the change of the parallel postulate of Euclidean geometry—lead to fundamental and massive revisions of the entire domain.

5. When a discipline or subdiscipline is new and there are only a few, say, ten, (more or less equally productive) contributors in it, each one engrosses a substantial amount of the whole (say 10 percent). So all of them count as really important contributors. By the time the field has grown to one thousand (again, more or less equally productive) contributors, each accounts for only 0.1 percent of the whole. None of them can compare in importance with those earlier contributors. Thus, the founding fathers of a field always loom larger in importance than their more numerous successors.

6. A starting point is provided by the books of Derek J. Price, *Science Since Babylon* (New Haven, CT: Yale University Press, 1975), and *Little Science, Big Science* (New York: Columbia University Press, 1963). An updated source is H. W. Holub, Gottfried Tappeiner, and Veronica Eberharter, "The Iron Law of Important Articles," *Southern Economic Journal* 58 (1991): 317–28. See also Jonathan R. and Stephen Cole, *Social Stratification in Science* (Chicago, IL: University of Chicago Press, 1973). The journal *Scientometrics* has published a great deal of relevant material in recent years.

7. The mapping of a citation space will, of course, need to be done in a fairly sophisticated way. If X cites Y and Y cites Z, then X's thus oblique citation of Z should be allowed to redound to Z's credit. And many other complexities also merit introduction.

8. Of course, to say this is not to deny that one cannot and should not be sophisticated in the use of citation statistics, for example, by giving greater weight to citations in articles that themselves are extensively cited. Again, the dialectic between what Derek Price called "archival citations" and "current citations" will have to come into play, since findings sometimes become absorbed or incorporated into larger ones and thereby drop from view notwithstanding their significance— a circumstance that would come into view only by looking at the "current citations" of the past. And even here one would want to distinguish between citations made on grounds of utility and citations made for the purpose of correctness. On these issues see Eugene Garfield, "The Obliteration Phenomenon," *Current Content* 51/52: 5–7; M. H. and R. B. MacRoberts, "Another Test of the Normative Theory of Citing," *Journal of the American Society for Information Science* 16 (1987): 151–72, as well as their "Problems of Citation Analysis: A Critical Review," *Journal of the American Society for Information Science* 40 (1989): 342–49; Derek de Solla Price, "Citation Measurement of Hard Science, Soft Science, Technology, and Non-Science," in *Communication Among Scientists and Engineers,* ed. C. E. Nelson and D. K. Pollock (Lexington, MA: D. C. Heath, 1970), 3–22. For further issues in the scientometrics of citations and citation analysis see *Scientometics* 43, no. 1 (1988), an issue devoted entirely to theories of citation.

9. Given that improbability is a matter of departure from the basis of existing knowledge, Laudan's criterion is not all that different from Popper's.

10. I am grateful to my colleagues at the University of Pittsburgh's Center for Philosophy of Science for fruitful discussion of relevant issues as well as to some anonymous colleagues who commented on a draft of this chapter.

CHAPTER 6: WHY PHILOSOPHY ITSELF MUST
BE SYSTEMICALLY HARMONIOUS

1. William James, "The Sentiment of Rationality," in *The Will to Believe and Other Essays in Popular Philosophy* (New York: Longmans, Green, 1897), 109.

2. Michael Dummett, "Truth," *Proceedings of the Aristotelian Society* 59 (1956–1959): 160; reprinted in *Truth and Other Enigmas* (Cambridge, MA: Harvard University Press, 1978). C. S. Peirce sometimes maintained a similar view.

3. This aspect of objectivity was justly stressed in the "Second Analogy" of Kant's *Critique of Pure Reason,* though his discussion rests on ideas already contemplated by Leibniz. See *Philosophische Schriften,* ed. C. I. Gerhardt, vol. 7 (Berlin: Weidmannsche Buchhandlung, 1890), 319–20.

4. John Kekes, *The Nature of Philosophy* (Totowa, NJ: Rowman & Littlefield, 1980), 196.

5. Some of these themes are also discussed in Rescher, *Metaphilosophical Inquiries,* chap. 2.

6. To be sure, its details must be wrapped in the intricacies of semantical theory. See Nicholas Rescher and Robert Brandom, *The Logic of Inconsistency* (Oxford: Basil Blackwell, 1979).

Index